3 MINUTES OF TRUTH
WITHIN 1,440 MINUTES OF LIES

KIM LANDGRAF

authorHOUSE®

AuthorHouse™
1663 Liberty Drive
Bloomington, IN 47403
www.authorhouse.com
Phone: 833-262-8899

Published by AuthorHouse 05/02/2023

ISBN: 979-8-8230-0683-5 (sc)
ISBN: 979-8-8230-0684-2 (e)

Library of Congress Control Number: 2023907499

Print information available on the last page.

Any people depicted in stock imagery provided by Getty Images are models, and such images are being used for illustrative purposes only. Certain stock imagery © Getty Images.

This book is printed on acid-free paper.

DEDICATION

This book is dedicated to the warriors who work tirelessly and at the risk of personal and professional repercussions, to bring truth and sensibility to the world. To those who spend their time and energy combatting the maleficence so pervasive in today's society. Those who have clothed themselves in the full armor of God and taken up their proverbial sword in this spiritual battle between good and evil.

I appreciate everyone who joined me on those Tuesday night council meetings and used their voice to shed light in the darkness. I met some wonderful people and am proud of and grateful for the friendships that ensued.

AUTHOR'S NOTE

This book is a compilation of poems/short stories/speeches written and presented by myself at my local county council meetings during the years officially known as the "Covid Pandemic" (more aptly named the "Covid **Plannedemic"**). Everything I've written is based on research, the research the MSM tries so desperately to censor. These works are my response to the lies and propaganda being force fed to the world. Some of these works are humorous, others take a serious tone. It is my hope that those caught in the snares of deceptive corporate captured journalism will read through these and take it upon themselves to search for the truth. I was given three minutes to speak. Here is my collection of three minutes of truth within 1,440 minutes of lies.

Contents

A VERY LIBERAL LULLABY 1

ABORTION PROCEDURES 3

CAMP L.I.S.A. 5

CAMP W.E.E.D. 7

CHRISTMAS JINGLES 9

COMMON SENSE 11

COUNCIL TYRANTS 13

COVID FACTS 15

COVID SHOT 17

COVID'S TRICKY 19

D AND C 21

DANGERS OF ABORTION 23

DIED SUDDENLY 25

DO NOT COMPLY 28

DO YOU SEE ME? 32

DRUNK ON POWER 34

EVERY CHILD HAS WORTH 36

FASCISM 38

FIGHT FOR YOUR RIGHTS 40

FREEDOM OF SPEECH 41

GLOBALISTS' PARADISE 42

HOW LONG? 44

HYPOCRISY 47

JAB MANDATE 48

JUNE 2022 50

JUST 8 BLOCKS AWAY 52

KELLI'S RANT 54

MASKS! 56

OPEN YOUR EYES 58

P.A.G.E. P.R.E.P. 61

QUESTIONS FOR THE COUNCIL 63

ROUNDING OUT '22 65

SEPTEMBER 2022- 1 67

SEPTEMBER 2022- 2 69

SOMETHING IS WRONG.................................. 71

Television......Tell-A-Vision......Tell-A-Story......Tell-A-Lie................. 73

THE CHOKEHOLD 75

THE CROOKED COUNTY COUNCILMAN............... 77

THE DATING GAME: MARXIST EDITION 79

THE DEMOCRATIC ABYSS 82

THE END OF THE WORLD AS WE KNOW IT 85

THE GATES OF HEAVEN 87

THE K.E.L.L.I. INSTITUTE 88

THE LAST TWO YEARS 90

THE LEFTIST PLAYBOOK................................. 93

THE ROOM NEXT DOOR 96

THE SCAM 98

THE YOUNG AND THE CLUELESS- episode 1 101

THE YOUNG AND THE CLUELESS- episode 2 103

THEN THEY CAME FOR MY VOICE..................... 106

Thump-thump......thump-thump 108

THUMP......THUMP......FLATLINE....................... 111

TO FLATTEN THE CURVE................................. 113

TRUTH 115

VAX ME PFIZER ONE MORE TIME 118

WAKE UP... 120

YOU KNOW YOU'RE A LIBERAL WHEN 122

ZEE IMPREGNATOR.. 124

A VERY LIBERAL LULLABY

Lullaby and good night
You were once my insignificant parasite
Now in neutral outfits so tender
So you can later decide your gender
Lay you down now in your mask
Is it safe, I didn't ask
Lay you down now in your mask
Is it safe, I didn't ask

Delightful dreams make you less grouchy
Turn not to prayer, worship Dr. Fauci
Silence those who disagree
Destroy this land, the land of the free
Lay you down now, let's be quick
You'll always be my little Bolshevik
Lay you down now, let's be quick
You'll always be my little Bolshevik

Lullaby and good night
I will fill your heart with spite
To be indoctrinated in your classes
So to fall in line with the masses
Soon committing violent acts
Reacting to feelings over facts
Soon committing violent acts
Reacting to feelings over facts

Sleepyhead, close your mind
Your birthing person is right here beside you
I'll offer you no protection from harm
As I don't believe in a firearm
You will never live in peace
As we've defunded the police
You will never live in peace
As we've defunded the police

Lullaby and don't you frown
You'll soon be burning our cities down
Daddy Soros will keep you out of jail
Replace your intellect with a Molotov cocktail
Rest your eyes now before the dawn
Victimhood makes you the perfect political pawn
Rest your eyes now before the dawn
Victimhood makes you the perfect political pawn

ABORTION PROCEDURES

Many Democrats and certainly the ones on this council have expressed their support for pre-born homicide, commonly known as abortion. For those Democrats who have never personally witnessed an abortion or are not knowledgeable to the different types of abortion procedures, I will explain them to you:

SUCTION ASPIRATION

The most common method during the first twelve weeks of pregnancy. General or local anesthesia is given to the mother and her cervix is quickly dilated. A suction curette (hollow tube with a knife-edged tip) connected to a vacuum machine by a transparent tube is inserted into the womb. This vacuum has a suction almost 30x more powerful than a household vacuum cleaner. It tears the baby and placenta into small pieces which are sucked through the tube into a bottle and discarded.

DILATION AND CURETTAGE (D & C)

Similar to the suction method with the added insertion of a hooked-shape knife (curette) which cuts the baby into pieces. The pieces are scraped out through the cervix and discarded.

DILATION AND EVACUATION (D & E)

Used up to 18 weeks gestation. Instead of the loop-shaped knife used in D & C abortions, a pair of forceps is inserted into the womb to grab the baby. The teeth of the forceps twist and tear the bones of the unborn child. The process is repeated until the baby is totally dismembered and removed. Usually the spine must be snapped and the skull crushed in order to remove them.

PROSTAGLANDIN CHEMICAL ABORTION

These chemicals cause the uterus to contract intensely, pushing out the developing baby. The contractions are more violent than natural contractions, so the unborn baby is frequently killed by them- some have even been decapitated. Many, however, have also been born alive.

SALT POISONING (SALINE INJECTION)

Used after 16 weeks when enough fluid has accumulated. A long needle injects a strong salt solution through the mother's abdomen into the baby's sac. The baby swallows this fluid and is poisoned by it. It also acts as a corrosive, burning off the baby's outer layer of skin. It normally takes over an hour for the baby to die from this. Within 24 hours, labor will usually set in and the mother will give birth to a dead or dying baby. There have been many cases of these babies being born alive. They are usually left unattended to die.

PARTIAL-BIRTH ABORTION

Guided by ultrasound, the abortionist grabs the baby's legs with forceps.
The baby's legs are pulled out into the birth canal.
The abortionist delivers the baby's entire body, except for the head.
The abortionist jams scissors into the baby's skull. The scissors are then opened to enlarge the skull.
The scissors are removed and a suction catheter is inserted. The child's brains are sucked out, causing the skull to collapse. The dead baby is then removed.

HYSTEROTOMY OR CESAREAN SECTION

Used mainly in the last three months of pregnancy. The womb is entered by surgery through the abdomen wall. The technique is similar to a Cesarean delivery except that the umbilical cord is usually cut while the baby is still in the womb, thus cutting off his oxygen supply and causing him to suffocate. Sometimes the baby is removed alive and simply left in a corner to die of neglect or exposure.

For Dr. Page, does this sound like First Do No Harm? For all the Democrats on this council, how in the world are you ok with promoting the torture and murder of a child in the womb? With a child being burned alive, torn apart limb by limb, or having scissors rammed into the back of its head? Being silent, dismissive, and accepting of these horrors reveals not only a darkness in your heart but makes you as complicit as the abortionist holding the scissors.

CAMP L.I.S.A.

Freedom of speech, so important that it is a constitutionally protected right. It is what guarantees my right to speak here tonight and it even guarantees Lisa and Kelli's right to extol the virtues of the socialist agenda. And I am fine with that. Everyone has the right to speak their mind, no matter how wrong they may be. The problem arises when they begin to implement those ideals. So, in an effort to educate through real world experience, I have brainstormed an idea to open up a "life under socialism" camp called **Liberally Indoctrinated Social Activists** or **Camp L.I.S.A.** for short. **Camp L.I.S.A.** will be dedicated to help reform young communists who have actually never lived under the oppression of a socialist regime, but praise its virtues anyway.

Upon arrival at **Camp L.I.S.A.** you will be greeted by a heavily armed member of the military whose top priority is your safety as evidenced by the miles long barbed wire border fencing surrounding our Gulag, I mean, camp. Several "for the greater good" health measures will be dictatorially implemented at **Camp L.I.S.A.** Once through the gates, a hermetically sealed face mask will be applied to each comrad's, I mean camper's, face; because a visual reminder of your submission is imperative to maintain group think mentality. Socialism distancing will be strongly enforced as meet-ups could prove a breeding ground for critical thought.

Group activities at **Camp L.I.S.A.** will include:
-An obstacle course wheelbarrow race, where you push wheelbarrows full of worthless bank notes to arrive at a state owned supermarket filled with rows and rows of empty shelves. Note that there are no winners in this race as equity is our primary goal. Even though you worked harder to get to the finish line before the others, doesn't mean you get the prize. It will be distributed equally among everyone, even those that chose not to push the wheelbarrow.

-Two classes for **Cooking under Socialism:**
1. **Fifty Seven Ways to Cook Dog Meat** and
2. **Fifty Seven Ways to Cook Beans and Rice**

-A financial course to keep you up-to-date on the current market price for organ harvesting in exchange for cash.

-Ways to pass the time as you wait in food and gas lines and then how to deal with your frustration when you get to the front of the line and the rations have run out.

-Mock elections; because it's fun to think that your vote matters!

Evenings will be spent sitting around a non CO2 emitting virtual campfire discussing climate change as if it really exists, watching state run news channels describing the evils of free market capitalism, and programming, I mean programs, explaining to you how fortunate you are to have the state looking after you.

There will be a short period before lights out when all comrades, I mean campers, in unison, will sing the **Camp L.I.S.A.** alma mater titled: "I Own Nothing and I am Happy, at Least That's What They Tell Me."

Ending your stay at camp will be a bit tricky as getting into **Camp L.I.S.A.** is much easier than getting out. Escape, I mean, departure tactics, may include: spoon tunneling your way out or building a makeshift raft to escape by sea. Whether you decide to stay with us or risk your life leaving, we promise that **Camp L.I.S.A.** will be an experience you will never forget! If you would like to see **Camp L.I.S.A.** become a reality please send your donation to
WWW.SOCIALISMONLYBENEFITSTHOSEINCHARGE.COM

CAMP W.E.E.D.

Have you recently escaped, I mean, finished your stay at Camp L.I.S.A. and are looking for a new camp to spend the rest of your summer? Do you have a degree in Social Work but not in Common Sense? Well, look no further because We Excuse Every Democrat is the place for you!

At Camp W.E.E.D we pride ourselves in the delusion that we can do whatever the heck we want without any repercussions. And this blind faith is the pillar for our three tenets of success:
corruption, unaccountability, and greed!

Our day at Camp W.E.E.D begins with a noon start time because, like, seriously, we're just too stoned, I mean tired to begin any earlier than that.

Our most popular day-time theme-filled activities include:
-Omission or guilt, how to tweak your financial interest statement
-Joint rolling 101
-How to lose total recall of a conversation
-Baking for edibles
-Why it's better to use a burner phone to avoid getting caught and
-Midnight cravings: are they cravings or are you just really hungry?

And because we know our campers **do** get hungry, food is available 24/7 in our newly renovated Cheech and Chong Cucina.

Nighttime will be spent staring at our hands, being fascinated with our moving fingers and singing the Camp W.E.E.D. Alma Mater: "My Political Career is Filled With Corruption and Greed, I Hereby Pledge My Allegiance to Camp W.E.E.D."

This year's honorary guest speaker at Camp W.E.E.D will be none other than Hillary Clinton, discussing her area of expertise: "If you can't delete the texts and emails, delete the people."

In order to maintain our illusion of acceptance, everyone is welcome at Camp W.E.E.D. But if you are a conservative, know that your attendance will be prosecuted to the fullest extent of the law. Per usual, our left leaning campers need not fear inculpation but, in the unlikely event of a raid, each liberal camper will be given a dark hoodie and instructed to "burn this camp to the ground!"

Though most instructional fees are covered by our beloved camp director G. Soros, there is a **one time camp fee** of $5,000 but, don't worry, that requires absolutely no paperwork on your part.

Locating our camp **is a bit tricky** as those darn conservatives don't want us within 1000 feet of any churches or schools, but, don't worry, with enough lobbying and pocket lining, we'll soon change that!

Though she normally doesn't have time for interviews, if you are interested in attending Camp W.E.E.D, please contact our founder Calisa Fancy at WWW.CORRUPTIONABOUNDS.COM

CHRISTMAS JINGLES

In the spirit of the season, I decided to tweak a few holiday favorites to better represent our current state of affairs here in St. Louis county and in the world today.

It's beginning to look a lot like mandates
Every time Sam speaks
Take a look in his eyes as he tries
To pass them once again
Flaunting the laws for the power that he seeks!

Grandma got run over by a reindeer
Walking back from the council Christmas Eve
Though, it won't be recorded as an accident
'Cause all deaths are labeled Covid to deceive

You're a mean one, Mr. Page
Two jobs, no one can squeal
Your ego knows no bounds, your destruction has been real
Mr. Pa-age
You're a crooked county executive
Before pharma you kneel!

Clancy tales, Clancy tales
Corruption all the day!
Oh, what fun as the tantrums start
When Lisa doesn't get her way-a

I'll be home for Christmas
Covid won't stop me
Please have D and plenty of C
And Ivermectin 'neath the tree

Faisal the con man
Should be fired, but likes to linger
He spreads his hate, such a nasty trait
And in the end gives you the finger

C-N-N, M-S-M
It's fake news time, in the country
Pfizer ties, hear their lies
They're all paid from big pharma's dime

Kelli baby
Slip a Tesla under the tree
For me
Fossil fuels are passé
Kelli baby
The polar caps are melting tonight

I saw Fauci kissing phar-ma stocks
Underneath the Wuhan lab last night
We all know that he's a creep
And considers us ignorant sheep
One day he'll go to prison
For his crimes they run so deep

Oh, the Marxists outside are frightful
But the Constitution is so delightful
And since there's nowhere else we want to go
Socialism's a no, it's a no, it's a no
Oh, the left don't show signs of stopping
And their policies are always flip-flopping
The school boards are corrupt, follow the dough
Socialism's a no, it's a no, it's a no

I hope you all have a freedom filled Merry Christmas and a Constitutionally
protected happy new year!

COMMON SENSE

Common sense, oh, common sense
Wherever have you gone?
Your presence here is greatly missed
From society you have withdrawn

All this talk of multiple genders
Just makes my head a swirl
I hate to break it, but God decided
If you're a boy or a girl

The Left is obsessed with pronouns and sex
With character development they are neglectful
Imagine how much better the world would be
If they'd identify as hardworking and respectful

And Leftist teachers intent on relaying
Who else lies in their bed
How about returning to academics
And teaching math instead?

Your sexual preference is not my kid's business
It's quite odd to be so assuming
You think you're helping my child to adapt
What you're really doing is grooming

School administrators distributing pornography
To kids in school is a crime
We need to get them away from our children
And sentence them to jail time

And men using women's bathrooms
Claiming their right to dress in bling
Guess what? My daughter has the right to use a public restroom
Without seeing their ding-a-ling

Hypocritical politicians who want to disarm you
Have armed guards at their discretion
They keep **themselves** and **their families** safe
But want **you** without protection

The source of violence is **not** the weapon
It's the **mind** behind the action
In their goal to remove 2A rights
They'll exploit race to gain some traction

They pump people with pharma drugs
Poison our air, our water, and our food
Then turn around and blame a gun
For the violence that has ensued

Mental health is an issue that's plaguing our country
And it's all by design from the Left
They indoctrinate our children with hate and intolerance
Because they themselves are morally bereft

Those on this council who affiliate Democrat
Just don't get you're pawns to this administration
Your minds, thus your actions are completely controlled
Your obliviousness is their foundation

You believe the CDC, FDA, and AMA all care for you
When corruption is all they resonate
They have since their inception been controlled
By the corporations they're meant to regulate

Your every reaction is in response to the media
Who are also controlled by the corporations
You need to start thinking for yourselves
And using critical thought in your applications

Take off your blinders, open your eyes
Try to be objectively observative
And if you really want to do what's right
Start identifying as conservative

COUNCIL TYRANTS

Here sits a county council
Who forgot they work for the people
They stole our God given freedoms
In order to control us like sheeple

Masks don't stop a virus
That's a fact and not fiction
Mandates only serve to feed
Their power hungry addiction

Some members are honest
Some members are not
But it's just a matter of time
Before we refill their slot

The people have awakened
And we are much the wiser
We know that King Page is merely
A puppet for Soros and Pfizer

But money is a great motivator
And has revealed true character throughout the ages
Now we clearly see who sacrificed
People for wages

The corruption in this world
Is really quite dire
You'd know a lot more
If you'd been watching The HighWire

Lisa and Kelli as you text back and forth
Praising the virtues of socialism
Realize your new I-Phones were obtained
Through the blessings of capitalism

Your socialist cries of a climate catastrophe
Are really oversteppin'
Try doing some research and look up
"What is a direct energy weapon?"

The women on this council
Will hang their heads in shame
Once they realize Page is using them
As pawns in his game

You are waging war against the people
By forcing them to comply
All the while knowing that injection
Could cause them harm and to die

Where there is risk
There must be choice
You rule through tyranny
To stifle our voice

You're taking part in genocide
All of you who push those vials
You will all be held accountable
Just like those in the Nuremberg Trials

We've given you facts week after week
We've tried to warn and tried to reason
But the crimes you are committing
Are by far nothing short of treason

COVID FACTS

For some reason, some of the members of this council do not care about facts.

The fact that Remdesivir killed 53% of participants in its Ebola trial. The fact that there are proven inexpensive preventatives and treatments being implemented by thousands of doctors worldwide (Vitamins A, C, D, Zinc, NAC, Quercetin, HCQ, and Ivermectin to name a few).

The fact that the vaccines cause viruses to mutate and become more virulent.

The fact that people are dying in hospitals NOT because of Covid but due to trickle down one size fits all treatment protocols implemented by bureaucrats that have their own agenda.

The fact that blood clots, myocarditis, sepsis, stroke, seizures, organ failure and **death** are all known side effects of these vaccines and are being swept under the rug and labeled as Covid deaths.

The fact that natural immunity is robust and long lasting.

The fact that these vaccines **do not** stop infection or transmission.

And the fact that this virus has an over 99% survival rate even when taking into account the inflated numbers propagandized by the corrupt mainstream media.

To the members of this council who voted in favor of a Covid vaccine mandate; is this the slippery slope of medical tyranny that you want for your own children and grandchildren, let alone yourselves? Do you really want to usher in an era of state mandated medical procedures, dissolution of the doctor/patient relationship, and loss of bodily autonomy for yourself and your family? Will you one day tell your children and your grandchildren that it is in part because of **you** that they no longer have control over their own health decisions and their own body?

What exactly is going on in your mind that makes you believe that you have the right to dictate a medical procedure for someone else? That you have the right to bully, bribe, and coerce someone to inject something into their body against their will? And just to be clear, injection without consent is medical rape and anyone who forces someone into that is just as guilty as the one holding the needle.

In case some people are not aware, Missouri has **Extortion and Coercion** laws in place.

In Missouri, extortion laws are covered by the statute that defines the offenses of "blackmail" and "coercion." These crimes involve making threats to reveal potentially damaging information or **threats to intimidate or place the victims in fear.** For county workers, the threat of losing their job, their livelihood, their dignity, and the opportunity to feed and shelter themselves and their family simply because they refuse the vaccine indeed intimidates and places them in fear.

If I was a county worker, I would be looking into this.

COVID SHOT

According to a press release from a Florida based Christian Legal firm, Liberty Council:

- All existing Pfizer vials (in the hundreds of millions) remain under the federal Emergency Use Authorization (EUA), meaning people have the option to accept or refuse.
- BioNTech received FDA approval for people ages 16 and above under the name Comirnity, but there are no Comirnity doses available in the United States.
- In other words, there is currently no FDA approved Covid-19 injection available anywhere in the United States. Every Covid shot in America remains under the EUA law and thus people have the option to accept or refuse them and
- Even when an FDA approved Covid shot becomes available, individuals are protected by federal law and many state laws from being forced to get these shots based on their sincere religious beliefs or conscience rights.

Ms. Webb, when you go door to door to bribe and coerce your constituents into getting this injection do you recite to them the list of possible side effects in order to obtain true informed consent? Side effects including but not limited to: blood clots, myocarditis, pericarditis, seizures, stroke, heart attack, autoimmune disease, cancer, and death? Or is your conscience allayed because you figure they can use their new $50 gas card to drive themselves to the Emergency Room?

Those facilitating this planned scamdemic have truly sacrificed their humanity. The Nuremberg Trials prosecuted those who committed the very human rights abuses and crimes that some of you on this council are committing today.

The Nuremberg code begins:
1. The voluntary consent of the human subject is absolutely essential. This means that the person involved should have legal capacity to give consent; should be so situated as to be able to exercise free power

of choice, without the intervention of any element of force, fraud, deceit, duress, overreaching, or other ulterior form of constraint or coercion; and should have sufficient knowledge and comprehension of the elements of the subject matter involved, as to enable him to make an understanding and enlightened decision.

I truly do not understand why this is so difficult for some on this council to comprehend.

Let this be clear: the truth **will** come to light, justice **will** prevail, and our Heavenly Father has already won this battle. The only questions remaining are:
Which side of history will you be on and where will you find your eternal resting place?

I'd like to finish with a few quotes from SCOTUS:

"A law repugnant to the Constitution is void. An act of Congress repugnant to the Constitution cannot become a law. The Constitution supersedes all other laws and the individual's rights shall be liberally enforced in favor of him, the clearly intended and expressly designated beneficiary." - _Marbury v. Madison, 5 U.S. 137 (1803)_

"Where rights secured by the Constitution are involved, there can be no rule-making or legislation which would abrogate them." - _Miranda v. Arizona 384 U.S. 436 (1966)_

"An unconstitutional act is not law. It confers no rights; it imposes no duties; affords no protection; it creates no office. It is, in legal contemplation, as inoperative as though it had never been passed." -_Norton v. Shelby County 118 U.S. 425 (1886)_

COVID'S TRICKY

Covid's really tricky
And seems to be unstable
That's why Covid disappears
When you sit down at a table

Here we are again for another meeting
For some this is a great interruption
We'd rather be with our families
Than calling you out on your corruption

But you leave us no choice
As your crimes run deep
How do you look yourselves in the mirror,
How do you sleep?

Masks don't stop a virus
By science's own admission
They only serve to fulfill the goal
Of psychological submission

You're depriving people of oxygen
Forcing them to rebreathe their own bacteria
A virus with an over 99% survival rate
Doesn't warrant this kind of hysteria

Worse than the fact that
Your jab mandate is illegal
Is the irrefutable fact
That it's killing people

Your cognitive dissonance
Is really getting old
You've surrendered your soul
For the lies you've been sold

You listen to the CDC and the WHO
Which are partially funded by Gates
A man whose goal is depopulation
And getting rid of people he hates

And evil Dr. Fauci
So filled with his own vanity
We know one day will be charged
With crimes against humanity

He warned an outbreak would happen
And clues he gave us plenty
Start by researching his patent
On Glycoprotein 120

You ignore those who've been exposed and recovered
Which is most in the community
If you'd follow the true science you'd know
Nothing trumps natural immunity

A thanks to three of the men on this council
Who understand with freedom you can't barter
Here's a shout of gratitude
To Trakkas, Fitch, and Harder

I left out Sam Page
A man who loves to gloat
A pro at squandering funds
And using Covid as the scapegoat

Sam was caught red handed
Someone snapped his picture and scanned it
Seems when he's out in public
He becomes the unmasked bandit

Perhaps the reason Sam's not here
And refuses to step foot on the council floor
Is solely because his ego
Won't fit through the council door

For those who vote for mandates
And make tyrannical demands
Rest assured you'll be held accountable
You have blood on your hands

D AND C

I walked into the examination room fully excited to see you again! Twelve weeks! That was a big deal! You now had fingerprints, could move your fingers and toes, smile, frown, suck, swallow, and pee! We may have even been able to tell your sex at that visit. But, that didn't matter to me. Boy or girl, I didn't care, I would have loved you just the same. I laid on the table as the doctor glided the ultrasound wand over my pregnant belly. After a moment I saw the happy look on her face turn contemplative. She continued to move the wand around several times and at different angles, all without saying a word, "Is something wrong?" I asked. "I'm sorry," she replied, "there is no longer a heartbeat."

Fast forward a few days. A few days lost to the surreal reality that this child I was carrying was no longer alive. That instead of proudly displaying his or her latest ultrasound picture and debating possible names, I now found myself standing in front of a triage nurse.

My doctor recommended I get a D and C to make sure all parts of the now deceased baby would be removed. As I approached the triage desk, the nurse asked me, "What are you here for?" "A D and C," I replied. "What's the reason?" she asked. "Miscarriage," I said. And in that moment her face went from what looked like a countenance of "I respect your choice" to "I am sorry for your loss."

How is it that that one word "miscarriage" was the difference between respecting a choice and mourning a life? How is it that my child's worth was determined by the reason for the procedure? That his or her worth was reduced to circumstance?

Was it not the same child?

That D and C was one of the most difficult things I have ever been through, both from an emotional as well as a physical perspective and I have immense sympathy for any woman who undergoes this because she was coerced into abortion and made to believe that the murder of her child was the answer to her trauma.

The reality of the matter is, that procedure did not erase my pregnancy. It removed that child from my body, but I will always be a parent to that child. And after sixteen years I still feel the pain of that loss. That child was a part of me. Every cell of my body reacted to that pregnancy. Its imprint can not be erased. Just as an abortion does not erase a pregnancy, it merely terminates it. At the moment of conception, the woman and the man become parents. Abortion does not change that, it just makes them parents to a dead child.

DANGERS OF ABORTION

Well, ladies, it seems that months and months of incessant mask wearing has finally brought to fruition what many of us have feared. Low oxygen and high CO_2 levels have gravely affected not only your cognitive abilities, but your common sense and empathy as well. I am referring, in part, to your vote last week regarding reproductive freedom. I feel compelled to inform you that reproductive freedom is choosing whether or not to take the pill, have an IUD placed, use a condom, etc.. It **IS NOT** the murder of an unborn child.

Lisa, isn't it weirdly and disturbingly ironic that the **"fight of your life"** as you called it, manifests itself through an unborn child losing the **"fight of his or her life"** through abortion?

And the hypocrisy, oh, the hypocrisy of you ladies knows no bounds. You shout bodily autonomy when it relates to abortion and in the same breath demand mask and jab mandates. My body, my choice, but only when it fits the agenda, right?

Since you ladies have failed to do any independent research as evidenced by the past year and a half, I went ahead and did some for you. Here are some facts regarding abortion that you are probably not aware of:

- The British Journal of Psychiatry found an **81% increased risk** of mental trauma after abortion.
- A study of California Medicaid patients found that the risks of suicide increase by **154%** for women after they have an abortion.
- Teen girls are up to **10x more likely** to attempt suicide then their counterparts who have not had an abortion and **4x more likey** to successfully commit suicide.
- Women who have had an abortion are **34% more likely** to develop an anxiety disorder.
- **110%.** That's the increased risk of alcohol abuse in women who have had an abortion.
- Women who had abortions **were more likely to die within ten years after their abortions** than women who carried to term. **Suicide** was a common cause of death for these women.

Psychological trauma is not the only consequence of abortion, **physiological consequences** follow as well:

- Women who underwent an induced abortion had a **50% greater chance** of developing **breast cancer** than women who had not previously aborted.
- A woman with a family member with breast cancer who had her first abortion after 30 years **increased her risk 270%.**
- The risk of breast cancer increases **significantly** with each abortion.
- A marker gene associated with breast cancer, **1NT2,** was shown to be **eighteen times higher** than the normal rate among those who had aborted.
- A number of studies done in the past 20 years indicate the existence of an **increased risk** of **cervical and ovarian cancer** where there has been a history of induced abortion.
- The risk of **colon and rectal cancer was up to 72% higher** for women who had had abortions than for women who carried their pregnancies to term.
- There is a **threefold increase in death** among infants born to mothers who have had a previous abortion as well as an increased risk of those mothers delivering a baby with **cerebral palsy.**
- The relative risk of ectopic pregnancy was **doubled** for women who had undergone induced abortions.
- Infectious complications of abortion include: Adult Respiratory Distress Syndrome, septic shock, renal failure, abscess formation, septic emboli and even death.
- 9.5% of post-abortive women need blood transfusions after **excessive bleeding.**
- The maternal death rate after abortion is more than **three times greater** than the maternal death rate after childbirth.

I was not aware of these facts until **I DID THE RESEARCH**. Which of you ladies were aware? Any of you? Does this truth matter to **any** of you? You ladies champion yourselves as warriors for women, yet the reality is you are placing women in grave danger by remaining oblivious to the very real psychological and physiological damages incurred by abortion. Get off your high horse and join the rest of us in **DOING THE RESEARCH.**

DIED SUDDENLY

When reading through the Sam Page interview in *West News Magazine* I actually laughed out loud at what I thought was an April Fool's joke by Page. The reporter asked Sam Page what he would do differently should another pandemic arise. Part of his response was that he would: listen to the experts, follow the data, and make decisions accordingly. This was a ludicrous response as during Covid Sam Page did NOT listen to the experts, he listened to the corporations. He did NOT follow the actual data, he followed the cooked data.

Over the past two years, myself and many others provided this council with references to the ACTUAL data; references to many independent medical doctors and scientists who stepped outside of the corrupt mainstream medical establishment because they could no longer bare the fraud, greed, and revolving door policies between pharma and the so-called "health experts."

And now due to the coercion, bribery, and mandates carried out by Democrats like Sam Page and those on this council we have exploding numbers of Covid shot related serious adverse events and deaths.

There are thousands of people, young and old, worldwide **dying suddenly.**

Do a search for **"Died suddenly"** and you will be horrified at the results.

"Blood clot, heart stopped, blood clot, heart stopped, blood clot....heart stopped"

"Died suddenly, died suddenly, died suddenly....died suddenly"

Are you, Sam Page and the Democrats on this council, proud of being "yes men and women," spinelessly towing the party line, having your actions dictated by the purse strings of the powers that be at the expense of St. Louis county?

The dangers of these mRNA vaccines have been known since their inception. The Pfizer data was available for you to read through, Dr. Page. And I use the term, "doctor," loosely because I have no respect for you as a doctor. You used your title and your influence in the medical profession to bribe, coerce, and manipulate people into taking an experimental bio weapon. That is despicable behavior that should call for your license.

By refusing to acknowledge the factual data, you and the Democrats on this council are complicit in the "died suddenly" occurrences happening worldwide.

You and the Democrats on this council did no research on masks, no research on this injection, no research on the effects of shutting down schools, no research into the detrimental emotional and mental toll forced isolation would have on adults and children in our community.

You did no research.

You mandated recommendations by the CDC, a for-profit organization well known for its corporate capture and who themselves admit that none of the vaccines on the childhood schedule have been tested for their synergistic effect on children. Translation: they have absolutely no idea how all these shots in combination are affecting the health of our children.

You listened to the advice of the maniacal sociopath that is Dr. Fauci. A monster of a man who signed off on torturing beagle puppies and carried out horrific and deadly experiments on orphan babies and children with his AIDS drug AZT.

The people of St. Louis County cannot afford four more years of the disastrous corporate/pharma influenced ruinous policies of Sam Page and his "yes men and women."

Their insidious behavior over the last few years went well noticed and when all truths come to light, I am hopeful that everyone who played a part in this **plannedemic,** this redistribution of wealth, this contrived economical/societal collapse toward a WEF sponsored global agenda, from council members, county executives, slimy politicians, health department personnel, scientists, doctors, nurses, pharmacists and anyone in between who pushed masks, who pushed and injected these clot shots, who shuttered and bankrupted small businesses, who turned a blind eye to the mental health of adults and especially children will be held financially and criminally responsible.

There is no, "I was just following orders." Everyone involved is culpable of crimes against children/crimes against humanity and **we will not forget.**

DO NOT COMPLY

I reached for my granddaughter Lilly's hand as we neared the border of our Fifteen Minute City. Immediately, my eyes cast a reflexive upward glance at the towering, cold, gray, concrete wall set before us; an intimidating representation of our forced compliance. I facetiously quipped to myself how ironic it was that they refused to build a wall to keep criminals, drug cartels, and human traffickers out, but were all too eager to build a wall to keep us in.

"Look grandma!" Lilly exclaimed, "It's the Wall of Protection. My teacher told me it keeps us all safe and stops the planet from dying."

I looked down at Lilly, her eyes vacant of wonder and curiosity; her gullible mind force fed globalist directed socialist propaganda.

I wanted to tell her, "I'm so sorry, Lilly. I'm so sorry you'll never know the freedom I had as a child. The simple pleasure of running a lemonade stand, of selling your old toys at your mom's garage sale and receiving cash to spend on a new toy or some candy." No, now every transaction is tied to digital currency and a social credit score which rewards or punishes you for how well you follow the global government's rules.

I wanted to tell her, but I knew we were being watched, we were being recorded. Freedom of speech murdered long ago by an incremental, methodical strangulation at the blood stained hands of bought and controlled bureaucrats. I looked to my left and saw the U.N. soldier slowly making his way towards us.

"Chip or phone comrade?" he inquired of me.

I had to answer or face incarceration. "I have a phone, my granddaughter has a chip." I replied.

He began scanning the implanted chip in Lilly's forehead as I retrieved my phone from my jacket pocket.

"Why is this child not at Instruction today?" the soldier asked.

I expected this question as, normally, Lilly would be at the UN Collective Elementary Education Center.

Lilly's parents, or co-caregivers, were both at their assigned work place. Staying home to raise a child greatly reduces one's social credit score so, in order to retain housing and acquire food, both co-caregivers must work while their children amass hours of programming, learning whichever version of history will benefit the New World Order.

"It's my last day and I was granted time with my granddaughter." I answered as I handed him my phone.

"My last day," I repeated inside my head.

I have been sick for a while now and it was decided by Leadership that I am a drain on resources as my production to consumption ratio has fallen below the sustainable threshold. For all their intents and purposes, I am no longer a benefit to society.

He seemed content with Lilly's scan, but his eyes locked mine after he scanned my phone.

"Comrade," he stated as he returned my phone, "your appointment at the For the Greater Good End of Life Center is in thirty minutes. It's best you get the little one back to Instruction so you are not late."

I nodded my head in acquiescence as I gathered Lilly's hand.

Sadly, to her, being detained by a soldier was commonplace and accepted. Her "normal" is the result of a previous generation's submission.

A previous generation who all too blindly followed the scripted narrative, easily manipulated into surrendering their freedoms as the "noble" thing to do. Not realizing that their fear, cowardice, and lack of critical reasoning secured shackles upon the feet of their own children and grandchildren. That when they allowed their voices to be censored and erased they rendered themselves inconsequential.

To Lilly, personal liberty is as foreign as what lies beyond that concrete border.

"I'm hungry, grandma, do you have any more cinnamon crickets?" Lilly asked.

I couldn't tell her the truth. That my rations ran out. That as I am now slotted for euthanasia, my food credits have been erased. So, I merely replied, "No, I'm sorry, honey, I left them at home."

I relished this moment, the last minutes I would spend with my granddaughter.

I held her hand as securely as a castaway lost at sea would clutch a piece of driftwood, saving themself, albeit momentarily, from inevitable death.

As we reached the doors to the Education Center, I lowered my head to Lilly's ear and whispered, "Goodbye, Lilly, grandma loves you. I'll see you soon."

Then, on instinct, a voice from deep within my soul quelled up in a desperate plea, a last attempt to impart a warning, as the words, "Do not comply" found passage through my lips.

Lilly looked at me in momentary bewilderment as the chip implanted in her brain began sorting through and erasing what it considered "dangerous propaganda." I knew that by tomorrow her memories of me would be gone anyway, as all memories of those departed are deemed useless. I would be fully erased during her next sleep cycle.

Within seconds her countenance changed. She smiled and waved goodbye as she turned to enter through the steel doors.

I turned around and looked at my watch. They were expecting me in ten minutes at The End of Life Center. I could drop my phone and run and hide, in a vain attempt to escape my fate, but I knew they would eventually find me. They always find you. And those who do not go voluntarily are slowly tortured to death, sometimes over days. If I go in on my own accord, I am promised a quick, painless death.

Suddenly, a loud beeping sound emanated from my phone. I pulled it out of my pocket and upon reading the word ALARM, was expelled from my sleep.

"Oh, my gosh, it was just a dream!"

I had been napping in the middle of the day. I noticed the time and quickly got ready. Tonight was my local county council meeting and I didn't want to be late. I planned on speaking about our freedoms being under attack and how global policies need to be addressed at the local level because if we turn our backs to trickle down politics, we become enslaved to them.

I made it to the meeting and sat until my name was called. As I reached the podium and began my speech, a voice of tyranny reigned down from the dais as I heard the words, "Excuse me, Miss Kim, I'm going to cut you off right there and give you a warning...."

And the voice of my future granddaughter whispered in my ear, "Do not comply."

DO YOU SEE ME?

Pedophilic symbolism is everywhere. It is especially prominent in Disney's movies and various merchandise. Child sex trafficking rings have been exposed at Disney World. Disney cruise ships traveled to Little St. James, better known as Jeffrey Epstein's 'Pedophile Island'. Many trafficked kids are sexual commodities obtained for and provided to politicians, government employees, celebrities, and people running and within corporate entities. Your children are being groomed in plain site. Groomed children are at a higher risk of being sexually exploited.

DO YOU SEE ME?
DO YOU SEE ME?
I'M A CHILD BEING TRAFFICKED
DO YOU SEE ME?

I was brought up from Guatemala and given to a man who would later pose as my father to make his entry into the U.S. easier. Another girl from my village was also brought up. Once across the border, I was returned to my trafficker to be sold again to facilitate another's entry. The other girl's fate was different. She was handed off to strangers and forced into prostitution and child pornography. She remains in the U.S. and is being held against her will, driven from appointment to appointment to have sex with men. She sees 15, 20 men in an evening and all money is being handed over to the trafficker. Biden's policy of releasing families and unaccompanied minors within 72 hours facilitates traffickers posing as parents in gaining entry into the U.S. Biden also eliminated DNA testing on adults and children traveling together that would ensure they are related to each other, making it easier for traffickers to get children across the border and sell them into the child pornography and sex slave industries.

DO YOU SEE ME?
DO YOU SEE ME?
I'M A CHILD BEING TRAFFICKED
DO YOU SEE ME?

I was brought into town for the Superbowl. This event is a magnet for human trafficking. He'll take me somewhere, maybe into a crowded hotel. No one bats an eye. Crowds of people, everyone partying, no one's paying attention. No one notices that I'm too young to be with this man. He's not my father. I was sold to him for a price. He'll rape me and beat me. He made it clear, if I cry out, he'll kill me. I don't know if he'll keep me or pass me around to his friends. I'm in the room next door to yours.

DO YOU SEE ME?
DO YOU SEE ME?
I'M A CHILD BEING TRAFFICKED
DO YOU SEE ME?

Elective abortion. Birthed in a water bag. In the world of child organ trafficking, abortion is a profitable industry where the sum of my parts is worth more than my whole. My organs will be sold and used for vaccine development, cosmetics, flavor enhansers for foods, and in some cases, scientific research that includes scalping 5 months gestation aborted babies and implanting their scalps onto rodents. In order to obtain viable tissue for commerce, I must be born alive with a beating heart. Without administering anesthesia, the abortionist will use the scalpel to slice into my face, into my skull, through my chest, and through my abdomen. They'll remove my liver, heart, brain, kidney, and bladder. The stainless steel glides through my delicate skin like a hot knife through butter. My silent scream is heard by God, ignored by man.

DO YOU SEE ME?
DO YOU SEE ME?
I'M A CHILD BEING TRAFFICKED
PLEASE SEE ME

I want to start out by saying what a complete and utter disappointment and embarrassment the beginning of last week's council meeting was. Observing Lisa Clancy was like watching a toddler who didn't get its way. Her behavior was extremely unprofessional and her palpable excitement at the thought of us all being escorted out by law enforcement was disturbing.

Watching a group of adults drunk on assumed power deciding whether or not they have the authority to muzzle another group of adults is beyond ridiculous. It was a clown show.

Lisa, it is both sad and humorous that the hypocrisy of your actions is lost on you. If you believe your mask works- WEAR IT. If you believe the injection works- GET IT but, you can't wear your mask, receive the injection and then feel threatened by others who do not worship at the altar of Fauci and Pharma as you do. It's like expecting ME to take birth control so YOU don't get pregnant. Your virtue signaling, "do the right thing" agenda floats atop emotions, not science. The narrative of "the only way to end Covid is to restrict your oxygen and receive a blood clotting injection" is falling apart and people are waking up to the politically and financially motivated BS.

Leave those of us alone who possess critical thinking skills and actually research the science.

Masks DO NOT stop a virus. The injections DO NOT stop infection or transmission but ARE causing blood clots, heart attacks, miscarriages, pulmonary hemorrhagic deaths of newborn infants to jabbed mothers, and serious injury and death to many others who've received it.

To those on the council who proposed and voted in favor of an injection mandate, the last thing that should be on your mind before you go to sleep is: Who and how many did my "yes" vote injure or kill today? Develop a moral backbone and repeal this mandate.

Each of you who voted in favor needs to be served with a notice of personal and financial liability for any and all injury and death resulting from this coerced injection.

And a quick interjection for Kelli. You do realize that the cobalt needed for your beloved electric car batteries are mined by hand by children as young as four years old in the Democratic Republic of the Congo. The working conditions for these children is atrocious. They work without breaks, protection or security in unbearable heat, digging at depths of 200 to 300 hundred meters and are at constant risk of asphyxiation, rockslides, or other accidental death.

Every charging station you mandate plays a role in child labor exploitation and abuse, but you probably didn't research this either, did you?

Seems your green energy requires a lot of little dirty hands to produce.

To all the women on this council and Sam Page:

SOCIALISM SUCKS!

And I hate to burst your bubble, but in a socialist society, role players like you are expendable and disposable to the 1%. Once you have served your purpose and they are bored with you, they will find someone else to push their agenda. To them, you are just another cog in the machine. The role players always go down for the crimes. So put away your copy of The Communist Manifesto and start reading, respecting, and following the U.S. Constitution.

EVERY CHILD HAS WORTH

Dr. Levantino, a former abortionist, became physically ill while performing a second trimester abortion, however he could not stop until the procedure was complete:

> "I looked, I literally looked at that pile of baby parts on the table, and I didn't see all the things that had sustained me all those years. I didn't see what a wonderful doctor I was helping her with her problem. I didn't see her wonderful right to choose, and I didn't even see the $800 cash I just made in 15 minutes. All I could see was somebody's son or daughter.
>
> Suddenly, this was looking really different to me. For the first time in my life it hit me very powerfully, that this woman had come to me figuratively and said...here's $800, kill my baby. And I was the type of person who would look right back at her very calmly, and say why sure, I'll do that.
>
> When you finally figure out...that killing a baby that big for money is wrong, it doesn't take you too long to figure out it doesn't matter if the baby is this big, or this big, or even this big, it's all the same."

A common theme among Leftists (and you ladies fall into that category) is that unborn babies are merely parasites sucking life out of the woman. With that in mind, I am curious at what point, ladies, did your own baby cease being a parasite and become a child? Was it before they were born? Right after they were born or a few years down the road?

Or is it only someone else's child that's a parasite and only if they are not wanted? Why is a child only valuable to you if someone wants that child? Can you really not see how selfish that is of you? Why do you believe your opinion is the deciding factor of a child's worth?

I couldn't even imagine telling my child, "Hey, buddy, you're only here because mommy decided not to have you killed and oh, by the way, you were once a parasite who magically became a baby when I was ready to call you a baby."

A 2005 National Geographic television program called "In the Womb" documents the development of the baby throughout the pregnancy and in the introduction sums up the scientific knowledge of the beginning of life as follows:

"The two cells gradually and gracefully become one. This is the moment of conception (fertilization) when an individual's unique set of DNA is created, a human signature that never existed before and will never be repeated."

When a pregnant woman is murdered along with her preborn infant, the assailant is charged with a double homicide, one count for the mother and the other for the baby. Sadly, when "choice" is involved abortion becomes nothing more than politically motivated murder.

And it is truly evil and pathetic that your immediate go-to for unwanted/ unplanned pregnancy is abortion. Never any talk of adoption/ counseling/emotional support/newborn training/things to help get a woman on her feet so she chooses life for her child. No, none of that. It's always straight to the killing for you ladies.

It's frightening to know that according to you, every child was once an abortion option.

It's frightening to know that your feigned concern for the woman ends as soon as the abortion is complete. You conveniently all ignore the possible future health consequences to the woman following abortion such as infection, septic shock, death, depression, anxiety, alcohol abuse, cancer, suicide, and subsequent babies being born with health issues.

No, none of that matters because you are all hypocrites towing the party line, sacrificing babies and women in the process. You should be ashamed.

FASCISM

The word fascism is being thrown around these days by the Left almost as much as their preferred pronouns. But, even their ignorance on that subject pales in comparison to their ignorance of what the term fascism actually means. The beginning definition of fascism begins with nationalism, or a love of country, a characteristic admittingly not possessed by the Democrats; so for arguments sake we will take out the word nationalism and focus on the rest of the definition:

A political ideology and movement characterized by a dictatorial leader (Biden), centralized autocracy (the D.C. swamp), militarism (the Covid police), forcible suppression of opposition (FBI), belief in a natural social hierarchy (the D.C. Elite), subordination of individual interests for the good of the nation and race (censorship), and strong regimentation of society and the economy (public school indoctrination, the Federal Reserve and the Green New Deal fiasco).

Well, what do you know, we just described the current Democrats, the progressive Leftists. We only have to look back at the lockdowns, suppression of individual liberties, forced medical treatments, renouncing of the U.S. Constitution, the 'we're all in this together, for the greater good, big government knows best' ideology shoved down our throats over the past two plus years. The 'wealthy off tax payers dollars' politicians who never lost a paycheck, sitting at home eating ice cream from their Sub-Zero freezers. The transfer of wealth during this time from the middle class and struggling mom and pops to the corporations lining the bottomless pockets of the elite politicians. The heavy hand and weaponization of the CDC, FDA, FBI, DOJ, and now even the IRS against We the People. How many times in Democrat-run counties, cities, and states were police called to remove those who wouldn't comply with the 'for the greater good' mask mandate? How many lost the ability to provide for their families, lost their health and their lives because of some egotistical, maniacal bureaucrat who decided they had the right to force an experimental bio weapon upon individuals? How many times were businesses padlocked at the behest of governors, mayors and county executives behaving like petty tyrants? Yes, indeed, it is the Democrats who are the fascists.

Ah, but there is that one thing missing: the love of country. Democrats have made it clear that their intent is to destroy the very foundation of this nation, to strip away individual liberties, to silence your voice thus erase opposition, tax you into oblivion, remove your right to defend yourself and your family, and micro-manage every aspect of your life; **to, in fact, dictate how you live your life.** Democratic policies are anti-constitutional, which makes them treasonous to this nation. Which is why I believe the Left are the true fascists, though they represent a new sect of fascism: **treasonous fascists.** Individuals with no love of country and no respect for the U.S. Constitution. Individuals who declare and impose edict after edict from their autocratic throne of hatred, hypocrisy, and greed. They send billions in aid to foreign nations while here in the U.S. our borders are wide open; with crime, homelessness, poverty, mental illness, drug addiction and depravity swallowing our cities whole. Many Americans are fighting to keep a roof over their heads, living paycheck to paycheck in a Democrat driven, unsustainable, inflation riddled economy. The Democrats are imploding this nation and their vision for this country is one of division and servitude where your children and grandchildren lay face to the floor under their boot of suppression. Remember this in November and vote these **treasonous fascists** out of office.

FIGHT FOR YOUR RIGHTS

This one's for the kids

Yeah!

Kick it!

You walk into your school, man, you **don't wanna go**
You cite the Pledge of **Allegiance**
But your teacher says, **"No!"**
You skipped CRT and Social Emotional Learning
And your teacher calls you out 'cause you're so discerning

You gotta fight
For your rights
And freedoms

Your classmates know you're MAGA and they say, **"No way!"**
But those lost Leftists have been led astray
Maaaaannn, life as a conservative can be so hard
Buuuut at least you don't live off your parent's charge card **(noble)**

You gotta fight
For your rights
And freedoms

You gotta fight

Don't step into this school, if it's a mask you won't **wear-er**
I'll kick you out of this class for **not using them/their**
Your teacher busted in and said, **"Silence that child!"**
Ohhhh, man that Union payoff has **you so defiled!**

You gotta fight
For your rights
And freedoms

You gotta fight
For your rights
And freedoms

You gotta fight!

FREEDOM OF SPEECH

"Congress shall make no law respecting an establishment of religion, or prohibiting the free exercise thereof, or abridging **the freedom of speech**, or of the press, or of the right of the people to peaceably assemble, and **to petition the Government for a redress of grievances."** Well, I've got some grievances.

Councilwoman Webb, I cannot speak for other members of the public, but I find your act of addressing constituents by their first names instead of their surnames blatantly patronizing. You stated these meetings are "business meetings," but your air of loftiness makes it feel more like Councilwoman Webb's Tuesday Night Preschool. We are not "we the people as controlled by Councilwoman Webb." It seems these last few years of apprenticeship under County Executive Page has molded you into his very own little "mini-me." Your demeanor is that of a self-appointed tyrant who has forgotten they are an elected representative. That means you were put in office by your constituents to work for them and to listen to ALL of their concerns, not just the ones on a particular night's agenda. Affronts to the U.S. Constitution such as this are exactly why I write speeches such as CAMP L.I.S.A. You, Councilwoman Webb, are pushing a socialist agenda of silencing free speech and playing it out in real time. You are marginalizing the very real everyday concerns of the people of St. Louis County. And just to clear things up, this is NOT a business meeting; this is government and government is about more than set agendas and wrapping up the meeting so you can get home. Governments and their policies determine very real consequences and affect lives and livelihoods whether they are typecast on an evening's agenda or passed years ago. Global and national policies trickle down and inevitably affect everyone. Your blatant disregard of our God given right to use our speech to air our grievances and voice our concerns, baffles me to no end. How in the world is this the life you want for yourself, your neighbors, and your loved ones? You are on the wrong side of history here, Councilwoman Webb, and I seriously hope your constituents are aware of what you are trying to pull because by silencing my voice, you are silencing theirs.

And lastly, in light of recent events, it is apparent the county will now need to appropriate funds to account for two salaries for Councilwoman Webb; one for her and one for her ego.

GLOBALISTS' PARADISE

As I walk through the valley of the Smart **City**, I'm **bereft**
Livin' my life, but there's no freedoms **left**
Complyin' and **cryin'** as the days drag **on**
My autonomy surrendered to sociopathic **morons**

An' the chip inside my head connectin' me to network **control**
Is **runnin'** software through my **brain, overridin'** my **soul**
Need to watch how I'm **talkin'**, which zone I can **walk in**
24/7 eyes on me **spyin', drones** my face **identifyin'**

Digital currency tied to social **credit,** makin' me a **supplient**
Forced to stay **compliant,** on their system I'm **reliant**
No more private ownership, everything's a **rental**
The self appointed **influential** decide **for me** what's **essential**

Been spendin' my life since 2030
Livin' in a Globalists' paradise
Didn't resist, now this hell feels like an eternity
Livin' in a Globalists' paradise

Regrettin' this situation I got myself **in**
Fallin' for the media's disinformation an' narrative **spin**
This mask silencin' me like a muzzle does a dog's **bark**
Servin' an' representn' my complete submission to the **hierarch**

Pharma controlled **chumps** with money on their **mind**
Mandatin' vaccines to commit genocide on **mankind**
Affectin' **fertility** by causing **sterility**
Autoimmunity, cancers, blood clots, heart attacks, strokes an' probable
disability

Gates dimmed the sun, now I've developed **rickets**
Can't eat meat no more, gettin' my protein from **crickets**
GMOs starvin' my brain/body of good **nutrition**
Promotin' drugs an' alcohol to limit my **cognition**

Engineered confusion, gender becomes **obfuscated**
The end goal, the family unit totally **annihilated**
Assistin' suicides, murderin' the **pre-born**
Schools openly advocatin' for young kids to read **porn**

Tell me why are we so blind to **see**
That the ones they hurt are you and **me?**

Been spendin' my life since 2030
Livin' in a Globalists' paradise
Didn't resist, now this hell feels like an eternity
Livin' in a Globalists' paradise

There's no climate crisis, only weather **manipulation**
It's a hoax an' a farce to push forced **regulation**
Everything electric is their ultimate **goal**
With a flip of the switch, they'll have you under **control**

DC launderin' our taxes through the **years**
Livin' the **highlife** off our blood, sweat, an' **tears**
Politicians an' bankers financin' manufactured **wars**
Spillin' the blood of young soldiers on foreign **shores**

They say I gotta learn, but they're never gonna teach **me**
Withholdin' education to keep me in **slavery**
Every election cycle makin' promises to **bait me**
Dividin' by **convincin' me** that my neighbor **hates me**

Been spendin' my life since 2030
Livin' in a Globalists' paradise
Didn't resist, now this hell feels like an eternity
Livin' in a Globalists' paradise

Tell me why are we so blind to **see**
That the ones they hurt, are you and **me?**

Open your eyes and finally **see**
Don't comply with these **fools** so your children can be **free**

HOW LONG?

Registered nurse Brenda Pratt Shafer recounts her experience watching a partial-birth abortion:

"I stood at a doctor's side as he performed the partial-birth abortion procedure, and what I saw is branded forever on my mind. On the ultrasound screen, I could see the heart beating….Dr. Haskell went in with forceps and grabbed the baby's legs and pulled them down into the birth canal. Then he delivered the baby's body and the arms-everything but the head. The doctor kept the baby's head just inside the uterus. The baby's little fingers were clasping and unclasping, and his feet were kicking. Then the doctor stuck the scissors through the back of his head, and the baby's arms jerked out in a flinch, a startle reaction, like a baby does when he thinks that he might fall. The doctor opened up the scissors, stuck a high-powered suction tube into the opening and sucked the baby's brains out. Now the baby was completely limp. Dr. Haskell delivered the baby's head. He cut the umbilical cord and delivered the placenta. He threw that baby in a pan, along with the placenta and the instruments he'd used."

To the Democrats on this council putting forth a resolution condemning the overturn of Roe v. Wade, do not have the gall to implicate all of St. Louis County in this matter. You DO NOT speak for me with this resolution. This is on each of you personally and needs to be worded as such.

Unlike you, I DO NOT condone the murder of unborn children.
Unlike you, I DO NOT mourn the **saving** of innocent lives.
Unlike you, I DO NOT celebrate the destruction of God's creation.
Unlike you, I am NOT OK with unborn babies being torn apart piece by piece, their body parts sold as commodities to the highest bidder and their rest tossed in the dumpster as useless trash.
Unlike you, I have morals.
Unlike you, I have ethics.

So, don't you implicate me in this matter.

How does it feel grandstanding for the murder of babies? No, I take that back. I don't even want to imagine the darkness that's in your heart for you to be ok with that. "Oh, but abortion is women's healthcare" you chant from your collective indoctrinated mindset.

Hmm....well, let's take a look at that.

Studies have shown that women who underwent abortions:

-Have a 50% greater chance of developing breast cancer
-Have an up to 72% higher increased risk of colon and rectal cancer
-Have an increased risk of cervical and ovarian cancer
-Have a 110% increased risk of alcohol abuse
-Are more likely to die within ten years after their abortions with suicide as a common cause of death
–Have a 3x higher risk of death than death after childbirth

Is this the "healthcare" you are talking about or is this the "healthcare" you **avoid** talking about?

I'm curious, will the funding you desire to get women to abortion clinics fund their chemo treatments as well?

Will it cover their funeral costs when they lose their battle with the cancer that resulted from having an abortion?

Will you be there to council the families of the women who committed suicide as a result of undergoing an abortion?

It seems abortion is not only a lucrative business for those profiting off the commerce of dead baby body parts (eyes on Planned Parenthood), but for the cancer industry, mental health industry, alcohol industry, pharma, as well as everyone involved in what ensues should a women die as a result of getting an abortion.

How sad and shameful that you place such little value, not only on a child's life, but a woman's life as well.

How sad and shameful that you put forth a resolution citing your displeasure that individual states can now limit pre-born child homicide.

How long until you hear their cries? How long until you hear their screams? How long until **THEIR** bodies matter? These children you so flippantly discard as dumpster trash.

How long?

HYPOCRISY

I am going to start off with a little quote from ClancyforStL.com (which I mentioned a few weeks ago, but I feel is important to mention again) : "Lisa has been a champion of Medicaid expansion, affordable quality early childhood education, fair wages, and paid parental leave- as well as your right to make the decisions about what happens to your body."

Next we move onto a direct quote from Kelli Dunaway: "As a fierce advocate for choice, I am dedicated to protecting every person's essential freedom to make personal decisions about their own health and family."

And in the words of Sam Page: "Every person has the right to reproductive health services and the freedom to control their own bodies, genders, sexuality, and lives as they see fit."

Any one of these three members who introduce and vote in favor of ANY legislation that limits a person's right to bodily autonomy such as mandatory masking or mandatory vaccination is both a HYPOCRITE and a LIAR.

Should one of these three members or any member on this council who has ever advocated for "my body, my choice" attempt to introduce any health legislation that infringes upon bodily autonomy, WE THE PEOPLE demand from these individuals a full retraction of ANY statements referencing such claims and a public confession and apology to their constituents for knowingly misrepresenting their political platform.

Data released on September 10 by the CDC showed that between December 14, 2020 and September 3, 2021, a total of 675,593 adverse events following Covid vaccines were reported to the Vaccine Adverse Events Reporting System(known as VAERS). The data included a total of 14,506 reports of death- an increase of 595 over the previous week.

There were 88,171 reports of serious injuries, including the reports of deaths during the same time period- up 2,200 compared with the previous week. According to a Harvard study, VAERS only captures about 1% of all injuries due to gross underreporting. A recent study at Mass General Brigham found that "severe reactions consistent with anaphylaxis occurred at a rate of 2.47 per 10,000 vaccinations." This is equivalent to 50 times to 100 times more cases than what VAERS and the CDC are reporting.

The idea of a Covid jab mandate, and I will call it a jab from here on out because it is NOT a vaccine but a gene altering experiment designed to turn your cells into spike protein producing factories, is horrifying. The idea that anyone could ever suggest such a mandate is abhorrent. Is this the slippery slope of medical tyranny that you want for your own children and grandchildren, let alone yourselves? Do you really want to usher in an era of state mandated medical procedures, dissolution of the doctor/patient relationship, and loss of bodily autonomy for yourself and your family? Will you one day tell your children and your grandchildren that it is in part because of you that they no longer have control over their own health decisions? Are you sure that YOU (once you get out of public service of course- because you, all members of congress and their staff and those in the federal court system are exempt from any jab mandate) really want that 15th booster shot because booster shot number 14 paralyzed the left side of your body? Well, that doesn't matter. No jab, no job, right?

What exactly is going on in your mind that makes you believe that you have the right to dictate a medical procedure for someone else? That you have the right to bully, bribe, and coerce someone to inject something into their body? And just to be clear, injection without consent is medical rape and anyone who forces someone into that is just as guilty as the one holding the needle.

At least we know that Ms. Clancy would not vote in favor of a mandate as she is, according to ClancyforStL.com (and I'm going to paraphrase here) "a champion of your right to make the decisions about what happens to your body." Right, Lisa?

And there's NO WAY Ms. Dunaway could vote in favor of a mandate because she herself stated "As a fierce advocate for choice, I am dedicated to protecting every person's essential freedom to make personal decisions about their own health and family." PHWEW! Thank you, Kelly!

And Sam Page would never suggest a jab mandate as he stated (again, I will paraphrase) "Every person has the right to the freedom to control their own bodies and lives as they see fit."

I am so grateful that these three have taken a public stance concerning bodily autonomy and personal liberty.

To the Democrats on this council, the Constitution was put in place to safeguard us from people like you. To keep the Shalonda Webbs, Lisa Clancys, Kelli Dunnaways, and Sam Pages of the world **in check.** Politicians who practice agenda politics which only serve to line their bottomless pockets and usher in Marxism. Politicians who errantly and arrogantly believe they have the right to strip away our God given freedoms under the guise of "it's for your own good." And stop, oh stop saying you care about the children or you are doing it for the children. It's a pathetic rhetoric incessantly used by the Left to sway public opinion by replacing common sense with emotion. People who care for the children don't:

- Advocate for their murder in the womb
- Jeopardize their health by forcing them to wear a mask all day
- Push experimental and dangerous biologics on them
- Shutter their parents' businesses thus stealing food from their mouths
- Limit their parents' right and thus their own right to self defense
- Look the other way as pornography runs rampant in schools
- Completely ignore the very real issue of child sex trafficking
- Stand idly by as our children are hyper sexualized
- Allow drag queens to expose their genitalia to children
- Constantly barrage them with sexuality so they're left confused, insecure, and depressed
- Allow a child who would choose ice-cream for dinner and still wears superhero pajamas, to take puberty blockers and have gender mutilation surgery

These are not things that sane people do, but the Left is far from sane and they are quite frankly a danger to our children.

This is why I propose the Left practice **S.A.F.E.** politics, as in **Stay Away From Everything** politics. Because literally everything they touch, they destroy. The Left is the hot dogs of politics; they package themselves to look like a good deal, but in reality they're just a bunch of cheap fillers, barely sustaining you and always bad for your health. They sow the same division they claim to stand against and use our hard earned money to form task forces to clean up the messes they create.

In order to reclaim the honor, dignity, respect, morality, ethics, and freedoms the Marxist Left has stolen and indeed continues to steal, we must all do our part in refusing their destructive ideology. One way is to return God and prayer to our schools and our nation.

On that note I will add a prayer that I wrote:

THE GATES OF HEAVEN

I don't pretend to know what's at the gates of Heaven or what judgment awaits me there
I only know the deeds I've done and the things I've asked in prayer

At times I've asked for abundance, placed too much value on wealth
Not appreciating the day to day and the simple joy that comes with good health

I've fought with my family, over many things inconsequential
Sometimes forgetting that it is our love that remains essential

I've tried to advocate for the unborn, to give voice to God's creation
Hoping to touch the hearts of those advocating for their assassination

I try to remain humble with the Holy Spirit as my guide
And refrain from committing transgressions under the guise of pride

I've fallen short on kindness on more than one occasion
Sometimes forgetting that selflessness is a big part of the equation

I hope the times I've done what's right
By far outnumber the times I'd lost sight

I hope I gave comfort every chance I was able
And shared food and drink from the bounties of my table

And when I led with my head thinking I was being smart
Jesus, please forgive me when those times broke your heart

I pray you wait for me at the gates as I navigate through my imperfection
And welcome me with open arms and the strength of your protection

For the only way to the Father is through you
Jesus, please guide me in all that I do

They've been trying for years. Hopefully tonight's the night. They're praying for a child.
Just 8 blocks away
They met at a party. They just really clicked. In the heat of the moment, they didn't use contraception.
Just 8 blocks away

Positive test. She glows from the joy this growing life inside her brings. As she strokes her belly a smile embraces her face.
Just 8 blocks away
Positive test. Her mind is at odds with her heart. She avoids her reflection in a hopeless attempt to stifle reality.
Just 8 blocks away

They go in for their first ultrasound. Their excitement is palpable. "It's a boy," the technician tells them.
Just 8 blocks away
She's been waiting to tell him. She hasn't seen him in months, maybe he'll be happy. She doesn't know where to turn.
Just 8 blocks away

They decorate the nursery with elated anticipation. Trains and trucks and teddy bears. They tell him all about it as she feels him tossing about.
Just 8 blocks away
She sits there thinking, "Am I doing the right thing? I have no one to help me. I can't do this alone," she reasons to herself.
Just 8 blocks away

They've been debating names for weeks. They'll name him after her grandfather. It's a good, strong name.
Just 8 blocks away
In a daze she walks through the clinic door. She's led into a room where the doctor inserts laminaria into her cervix to begin dilation. She's to return in 24 to 48 hours.
Just 8 blocks away

Her water breaks. "It's too early," she worries. "We'll do everything we can to save him," they reassure her.
Just 8 blocks away
She's back at the clinic. Her belly is cramping as she walks down the hall. "I don't want to do this," she whispers to herself as they place her feet in the stirrups.
Just 8 blocks away

Ten perfect fingers and ten perfect toes. Doctors and nurses working in concert to save this life. The sound of a tiny heart beating rivals the most beautiful of symphonies.
Just 8 blocks away
Ten perfect fingers and ten perfect toes with seconds left to live. Everything delivered except the head. The doctor rams the scissors into the back of his skull.
Just 8 blocks away

He's headed to the NICU but he'll be fine. He's strong for such a little guy. They bow their heads in prayer and gratitude.
Just 8 blocks away
His body goes limp. His head is pulled free, mouth agape in a silent scream. He's tossed onto a tray to be discarded as trash.
Just 8 blocks away

Both lives of equal value. Both precious children of God. One life began and another life ended.
Just 8 blocks away

KELLI'S RANT

And the award for the most uncompassionate, inhumane, immoral, unethical, maniacal diatribe based solely upon tired, group think liberal rhetoric goes to Kelli Dunnaway for her Oscar worthy rendition of **"IS THAT PRO-LIFE?"**

Anyone who actually takes the time to write a speech on why society should give a green light to kill babies has fallen so low on the depravity scale, there may be no reaching her. What kind of a person mocks the miracle of life? What kind of a person believes that a child's intrinsic worth and right to existence depends solely upon if that child is wanted or not? Of course, Kelli's unhinged rant comes as no surprise as she represents a political ideology that actively promotes violence.

Somewhere along the way, Kelli, you rationalized murdering babies. You rationalized babys' limbs being violently ripped piece by piece from their torso, their tiny heads being crushed, their brains being sucked out, their little bodies being burned alive and their beating hearts being abruptly stopped all in the name of "choice."

Since Leftists love to refer to the pre-born as "parasites", my question for the Leftists on this council is, at what point did your own children stop being parasites? Was it before they were born, right after, a few years down the road? Do you still refer to them as parasites because, in truth, they are in fact that same "clump of cells" they were when they were conceived. Are you even aware that, from the time a baby is created at **fertilization**, he or she already has all the DNA they will ever have?

Ah, but these children were **wanted** and it is only the **unwanted** children that carry the derogatory term of parasite, correct? Falling in line with the Leftist agenda of "our rules change as our narrative changes."

How **telling** that you advocate funding abortion centers and not pregnancy care centers. How **sad** that you do not believe that women deserve better than the **trauma of abortion.** How **pitiful** that you look the other way at the marked increase in breast, cervical, ovarian, rectal and colon cancer in women who have had an abortion. How **irresponsible** that you turn a blind eye to the increase in alcoholism, anxiety, depression, and **suicide** in women who have had an abortion. How **shameful** that your advocation and praise for murdering the pre-born supersedes your respect for women and their physical and emotional well-being.

So, I ask you:
-Will you be there for those women who receive a cancer diagnosis as a result of a past abortion?
-Will you drive them to and help pay for their cancer treatments?
-Will you help fund their funeral should they succumb to these abortion induced cancers as you advocated to fund their abortion **procedure?**
-Will you help those women who turn to alcohol to deal with the extreme anxiety and depression they feel after having an abortion?
-Will you be there to counsel the families of the women who committed suicide after their abortion just as you were those women when you counseled them to **get** an abortion?
-Will you let these women know that the maternal death rate after abortion is more than **3x greater** than the maternal death rate after childbirth?

As promoters of abortion, it is your responsibility, it is your ethical duty to inform women of these consequences. Failure to do this exemplifies what so many of us already gather from those on the Left: **that your support for women ends at the abortion clinic door.**

MASKS!

So, here we are again discussing masks! Now, I could stand here and reiterate what hundreds of doctors and virologists WORLDWIDE and numerous studies have stated for years: that viral particles pass right through a mask. That, in fact, viruses become aerosolized when passing through a mask (kind of like a spray bottle effect) and spread out FURTHER and WIDER. That wearing a mask not only DECREASES oxygen intake, but INCREASES CO_2 levels in your blood, thereby causing your blood to become ACIDIC which INCREASES your chances of developing and proliferating CANCERS, as cancer thrives in an acidic environment. That one thing masks ARE effective at is trapping BACTERIAL particles which then proliferate in a moist environment and become concentrated in your nasal and respiratory passages, making their way to your brain and your lungs (thereby INCREASING your risk of developing bacterial pneumonia). But those of us who have actually DONE the research, KNOW all of this. ACTUALLY, I think we are past this point in the discussion as cognitive dissonance seems to have replaced ANY critical thinking these days. My point today is based on the FACT that NO elected official has the right to dictate which medical interventions I or my children take. And, YES, a mask is a medical intervention as it produces not only PHYSIOLOGICAL changes in the body as I previously stated, but PSYCHOLOGICAL damage as well. Do you have any idea how difficult it is for some victims of domestic abuse or rape to wear a mask? Do they not matter to you? There are ABSOLUTE risks to masking up day in/day out for hours/days/months/ and now going on YEARS at a time. And where there is risk, there MUST BE CHOICE!

My health, my children's health is MY RESPONSIBILITY. Your health, your children's health IS YOURS. If you choose to mask up, mask your children up, cower in perpetual fear and not do any research regarding steps YOU can take to strengthen your immune system and mitigate your chances of becoming ill, that is completely ON YOU, as it should be. And if you truly believe that your mask is effective, then it should not be an issue if I do not wear one. YOU CAN'T HAVE IT BOTH WAYS. THAT IS HYPOCRISY.

I am literally ASTOUNDED at the fact that ANY elected official actually BELIEVES that they have a say over my or my children's BODILY AUTONOMY. YOU DON'T. And many realize that this is about more than a mask. The mask is merely a gateway to forced injections. Medical dictatorship has NO PLACE in a free society and I WILL NOT COMPLY!

OPEN YOUR EYES

Open your eyes
For heaven's sake, open your eyes
We are letting you know this scamdemic
Is really evil in disguise

Event 201
Was a dry run for this insanity
The end goal is to wipe out
90% of humanity

This is not about a virus
There's a much bigger goal
It's about enslaving the population
And keeping everyone under control

Rearranging the letters in Omicron
Spells out moronic
Wake up, you're being played
Yes, they're really that demonic

Madman Gates has already stated
"The next pandemic will get their attention"
He'd love to release smallpox
And sell you the prevention

Those who speak the truth
Face extreme censorship
If this was really about health, everyone would get
A free gym membership

Or how about high dose vitamin D
Which can cut viral deaths by 60%
Imagine all the sickness
Vitamin D could prevent

Ivermectin, Ivermectin
That's been proven to be a solution
Though all the good doctors prescribing it
Have been facing persecution

Fresh fruits and vegetables
Reaching people door to door
Would certainly make people healthier
Than they were before

But Sam remains silent
On the topic of nutrition
I guess that's what happens when pharma
Forces you into submission

Build Back Better
Is a globalist phrase from hell
That's meant to impose tyranny
And delete every last brain cell

Sam and his crew of commies
Tell us it's what we must embrace
It's real goal is to oppress you
Keeping you down with a boot on your face

At what point did Sam begin to lose his way?
When did he become such a traitor?
Someone please remind him, MD stands for medical DOCTOR
NOT medical DICTATOR

He pushes these shots
Even though they've proven to cause harm
If he had any ethics whatsoever
He'd be sounding the alarm

How dark and evil is the heart
Of those who sacrifice kids
All complicit in injecting these children
Are participating in what the Creator forbids

Sam, you're a doctor so I thought you'd know
The benefits of natural immunity
Instead you weaponize fear to divide
And invoke harm on your community

Repeating "safe and effective"
Doesn't make it the truth
Why aren't you concerned that it's causing
Myocarditis in our youth?

Injecting poison to produce health
Is quite the dichotomy
In order for that to make sense
You'd need a lobotomy

You and Faisal Khan
Each your own biggest supporter
You both should seek counseling for
Narcissistic Personality Disorder

Pornography in schools, suicide rates increasing
Crime's out of hand, jails are imploding
Get on the right side of history, Sam
Your credibility's fast eroding

We are a free people
From your tyranny we decline
We will not comply with your illegal mandates
You can stick them where the sun don't shine

P.A.G.E. P.R.E.P.

Do you lie awake in bed at night thinking, "I'm the best, I'm the smartest and anyone who doesn't agree with me should suffer the consequences?" Do you consider yourself a leader, but don't let your pride get in the way of being controlled by those above you? If this sounds like you, then **Possessing A Giant Ego Preparatory** may be the place for you!

P.A.G.E. Prep prides itself in molding young dictators into the leaders the world doesn't want, but will be thrust upon them anyway.

Courses at **P.A.G.E. Prep** include:
-Autocracy 101
-Rules For Thee, But Not For Me
-Wokeism: It's How To Get Things Done
-Dictatorships For Dummies
-Censorship Over Debate: The Leftist Strategy For Success
-Soros' Guide To Race Exploitation: How To Divide To Conquer
-57 Ways to Badmouth Your Constituents
-Socialism Psychosis: How To Brainwash the Masses
With the follow-up course:
-Easing into Socialism: One Mandate at a Time

Please be aware that all classes at **P.A.G.E. Prep** are videotaped, so putting on a good show, I mean, following the rules, is imperative. Of course, once the cameras are turned off, you are free to do as you please.

While enrolled at **P.A.G.E. Prep,** it is frowned upon to take classes at another institution, but as long as you don't get caught, we'll look the other way and pretend it never happened.

At **P.A.G.E. Prep** we firmly believe that the lack of differing opinions is crucial in manifesting the collective mindset necessary to usher in one world government control. That is why all courses are taught by one man: Dr. Ima Fraudci. Dr. Fraudci epitomizes all we hold near and dear here at **Possessing A Giant Ego Academy** and is, in fact, the only person in the world to hold a masters degree in S.U.I.K.E.B.T.Y.: Shut Up I Know Everything Better Than You.

All meals will be served in Bolshevik Hall by the working class who will never be allowed to come within touching distance of you, but will be required to tell you how fortunate they are to not have to think for themselves.

While boarding at **P.A.G.E. Prep** you will have the choice of two living accommodations: Lenin Lodge or Stalin Suites and, as **Build Back Better Off the Backs of Others** is our motto here, rest assured no blood, sweat, and tears were spared to accommodate the luxury you deserve as a future tyrant.

Recreational activities at **P.A.G.E Prep** include:
-Defacing and tearing down historical statues in an attempt to erase history and reform malleable minds.
-Practice drills for false flag events
-Group chats focusing on ways to destroy the nuclear family and how to better emasculate men.
-Weekly get togethers discussing ways to make **everything** offensive.

Evenings will be spent reading the Communist Manifesto and afterwards all students are encouraged to sing the **P.A.G.E. Prep** alma mater: "Do As I Say, Not As I Do or It's A One Way Trip To The Gulag For You!"

Not all who apply will be admitted to. **P.A.G.E. Prep.**, only those who truly have **DOMINION** over their own lives and ambitions will be **SELECTED**, but if you are willing to sell your soul for earthly treasures, please fill out our enrollment application at www.Imanegomaniac.com

QUESTIONS FOR THE COUNCIL

Over the past two years, the Democrats on this council have evinced more queries than answers. To that effect, I have compiled a list of several pivotal questions that I believe constituents deserve answers to and, in the spirit of transparency, should be shared on the council website:

1. Why do you so despise the basic principles and fundamental rights this country was founded upon?
2. What do you love most about tyranny?
3. Why do you favor communism over a Constitutional Republic?
4. Name the communist country you would most like to live in and why?
5. **Would you consider seeking memory retrieval therapy** to help unblock your recollection of the U.S. Constitution and the Nuremberg Code? **Because I would pay for that.**
6. Why are you not ashamed and embarrassed to align yourself with a political party so intent on systematically destroying the U.S. from within through corruption, division, and totalitarian government control?
7. Why do you support government sanctioned medical tyranny?
8. Do you honestly not realize that by dictating what I put **on and in my body** you are essentially declaring that you **own my body and that I belong to you** and that that belief categorizes you as a textbook example of a **controlling, abusive individual?**
9. Is it difficult to look yourself in the mirror after using coercion techniques and work related mandates to push an injection on adults and children that lists **severe autoimmune diseases and death** among many other side effects knowing that, through those actions, you are personally responsible should those outcomes occur? Do you sleep soundly knowing you've played a part in crimes against humanity and crimes against children?
10. Why, Sam Page, did you **not** follow your Hippocratic Oath and warn your constituents that face masks intended for the general public are sterilized with **carcinogenic Ethylene Oxide** and contain dangerous levels of **Titanium Dioxide, a suspected**

human carcinogen when inhaled? In your opinion, is lung cancer a good trade off for a virus with an over 99% survival rate?

11. Why, over the past two years, have you refused to acknowledge lifesaving **Ivermectin and HCQ** when doing so could have saved lives?

12. How do you plan to remedy the psychological damage your lockdowns, mandates, and isolation have caused many, **especially children,** and what assurances can you provide your constituents that your common sense and critical thought have been restored and you will never again override constitutionally protected liberties to satisfy your own lust for power?

13. What are your thoughts on The Great Reset/Agenda 2030 and what do you envision your role to be in that endeavor?

14. Do you align yourself with The World Economic Forum's plan of a one world government, digital currency, digital I.D., social credit score, abolition of private property, and transhumanism?

15. Have you ever had dreams featuring George Soros or Klaus Schwab where either one has uttered to you the phrase, "Who's your daddy?"

16. And, finally, at what point did you become so **arrogant and removed** that you believed you could **strip away an individual's right to govern themselves and their children, to make medical decisions for themselves and their children, and to deny themselves and their children the fruits of their labors?**

I look forward to reading your answers.

ROUNDING OUT '22

I thought I'd round out '22 with some facts and talking points. And, please, unlike the Corporate controlled lying mainstream media, I encourage you to research these things on your own. The only caveat is please do not rely on Google, as, first fact:

- Google has strong ties to the pharmaceutical industry. Meaning, they not only suppress information, but prioritize biased information
- When your doctor and the hospital say to you "standard of care" that translates to, "Whatever the medical cartel directs and allows us to do."
- Remdesivir causes kidney failure
- Ivermectin and HCQ are curative and effective, but were swept under the rug so that the jab could get Emergency Use Authorization
- On August 22, 2005, ***The Virology Journal*** the official publication of Dr. Fauci's NIH published an article under the heading **"Chloroquine is a potent inhibitor of SARS coronavirus infection and spread."** To quote the researchers, "We report... that chloroquine has strong antiviral effects on SARS-CoV infection of primate cells. These inhibitory effects are observed when the cells are treated with the drug either before or after exposure to the virus, suggesting both prophylactic and therapeutic advantage." Said Dr. Fauci's NIH in 2005, "concentrations of 10 micromolars completely abolished SARS-CoV infection." Fauci's researchers add, "chloroquine can effectively reduce the establishment of infection and spread of SARS-CoV."
- Never forget they forbade people from spending their last dying breaths with their loved ones for a treatable virus.
- Dr. Fauci approved HIV drugs which were toxic to adults, to be experimented on thousands of foster children (most of them black, hispanic, and poor)
- If the children resisted the drugs, they were held down and force-fed. If the children continued to resist, a surgeon at Columbia Presbyterian Hospital put a plastic tube through their abdominal wall into their stomachs. From then on the drugs were injected directly into their intestines

- According to Vera Sharav: "Fauci just brushed all those dead babies under the rug. They were collateral damage in his career ambitions. They were throw-away children."
- Watch the 2004 BBC documentary *Guinea Pig Kids* to learn more about this
- If a pregnant woman is shot in the belly and the baby dies, the assailant is charged with murder
- If that same woman enters an abortion clinic and the abortionist murders her child, that clinician faces no repercussions
- If you don't see the hypocrisy in that and instead assign value of life to circumstance, congratulations, you have successfully dehumanized yourself
- The DC elite do not have "kitchen table discussions" and they don't give a bleep about yours
- Democrats and RINOS are controlled by the World Economic Forum
- The Southern border is wide open and children are being trafficked for sexual exploitation throughout the nation while DC and the media remain silent
- Did we all just forget about Epstein's client list?
- The breaking news is always the distraction
- The term 'side effects' is used to sugarcoat what drug reactions really are: adverse events resulting from your body **responding to and attempting to detox from** the poisons you have ingested or injected
- Web search **Vaccine.guide** for access to vaccine adverse events
- Web search the **Vaccine Excipient Table** for vaccines and their ingredients

Resident Biden stated we are in a battle for the soul of the nation
And about that he is right
Conservatives pray to God for strength
While the Left aligns with Satan in this fight

The warriors of common sense and those who actually think
Realize Biden's Build Back Better schtick
Is a chokehold on the common man
An homage to a Bolshevik

Implementing communism via the globalist agenda
Democrats are a disgrace to our nation
Condemning us and future generations
To a life of servitude and devastation

The globalists plan for cash transactions
Is to have them completely barred
I can just hear future parents now
Oh, look, honey, the tooth fairy left you a debit card

When they control the money, they control you
Please exit, Miss Smith, you can't buy from this store
Your numbers are in the negative
On your social credit score

And ugghh, the Left's obsession
With teaching sex to our youth
It's time they stop pushing degeneracy
And start focusing on God's truth

Classrooms have become
The new unsafe space
Where kids are taught by indoctrinated teachers
To be ashamed and a victim of their race

Educators crossing the line
Explaining their sexuality at school
Filling kids minds with preferred pronoun nonsense
Hoping the kids find them cool

If you're an adult who looks to a child
For acceptance and affirmation
Either you're plagued with insecurity
Or focused on predation

It's time to talk about our own county council
And the members who lean Democrat
Often behaving like petulant children
Always wielding the mindset of an autocrat

Miss Webb, the Constitution now represents us all
How shameful that on this you cast such doubt
If you really despise living here so much
Please, don't let the border hit you on the way out

We know from your past council decisions
That individual liberty you do not respect
People lost their jobs and their bodily autonomy
Because your greed and ego went unchecked

Miss Clancy encouraging kids to read pornography
Should be a red flag for her constituents
Democrat or Republican, it's best to keep your kids
Far away from of her sphere of influence

Why she wants kids to read porn
Is overwhelmingly beyond my comprehension
Unless it's like most of her actions
Done solely for political attention

Like wearing a uterus t-shirt
And mocking the murder of the unborn child
It's sad her moral compass
Remains so utterly defiled

And miss Dunnaway, ever gullible
To the global warming hoax
Actually believes the corporate bought scientist
Screaming "We're all gonna die soon folks!"

For "green energy" is quite the money-maker
Just not for the ordinary prole
And SSHH for heaven's sake don't tell her
That electricity is powered by coal

And all those electric vehicles
For those who can foot the bill
Seems she ignores the fact that their batteries
End up in a biohazard landfill

Sam ignoring the Covid shot-induced myocarditis
And continually pushing to vaccinate every arm
Is violating the Hippocratic Oath he took
Of First Do No Harm

It's unfortunate Sam's allegiance to Pfizer
Has cast a shadow over St. Louis county
He's put politics before people
To share the rewards of big pharma's bounty

Oh, Sam, we see right through you
Your insatiable lust for power is a flawed character trait
Only a man adrift in the frailty of his mind
Lives his life to subjugate

Hopefully the day of restitution
Is soon on the horizon
And Sam's name will be duly replaced
For a prison bar code with a hyphen

So for now we live with this petty tyrant
Just don't lose hope and always remember
The only way to save our county
Is to vote him out in November

SOMETHING IS WRONG

When people are intentionally plunged into media driven panic and fear and economies are destroyed due to a virus with an over 99% survival rate,
SOMETHING IS WRONG

When thousands of doctors worldwide are successfully and safely treating and healing Covid patients with HCQ, Ivermectin, C, D, Quercetin, NAC, and Zinc but are silenced and threatened,
SOMETHING IS WRONG

When they've managed to convince the public that they were able to create and manufacture a life saving injection for a so called novel deadly virus within a year but, haven't been able to create a successful antiviral after decades of trying,
SOMETHING IS WRONG

When the media, politicians, and health departments turn a blind eye to the hundreds of thousands of people being injured and killed by this injection,
SOMETHING IS WRONG

When people lose their jobs, their relationships with family and friends, and their ability to enter public accommodations for defending their bodily autonomy,
SOMETHING IS WRONG

When the very politicians who are dictating mandates for you have exempted themselves,
SOMETHING IS WRONG

When informed consent doesn't matter anymore,
SOMETHING IS WRONG

When children's brains and lungs are being starved of oxygen by a bacteria ridden mask they are forced to wear all day,
SOMETHING IS WRONG

When liquor stores, box chains, and fast food are essential, but churches, mom and pops, and gyms are not,
SOMETHING IS WRONG

When they've convinced you that **you** are nonessential,
SOMETHING IS WRONG

When your liberties are stripped for "the greater good", but the "greater good" only seems to benefit those making the rules,
SOMETHING IS WRONG

When "defund the police" affects neighborhood patrols and community dispatch but, doesn't affect police protection of politicians,
SOMETHING IS WRONG

When politicians expect and depend on the brave men and women of the police force to protect them, even risk their lives for them, then turn around and tell them, "Guess what? You don't get to feed your family if you don't surrender your body to us and get the injection",
SOMETHING IS SERIOUSLY WRONG

We the people must come together and step outside of the divisional lines of politics, gender, religion, socio-economic standing and race manufactured and fueled by politicians and the media.

Masked or not
Vaxxed or not
White or black or brown or any color in between

IT DOESN'T MATTER

TYRANNY CANNOT SURVIVE IN THE FACE OF A UNITED PEOPLE
TYRANNY STOPS WHEN THE PEOPLE, TOGETHER, SAY IT STOPS

THEREFORE, WE MUST NOT COMPLY
AND WE MUST NOT SURRENDER
OR ELSE OUR GRANDCHILDREN WILL NEVER KNOW
THE FREEDOMS WE REMEMBER

Television......Tell-A-Vision......Tell-A-Story......Tell-A-Lie

Event 201, October 2019. Showing the world what's to come. A simulated Coronavirus pandemic. Funded by The World Economic Forum and The Bill and Melinda Gates Foundation. Two organizations that favor depopulation.

Television......Tell-A-Vision......Tell-A-Story......Tell-A-Lie

People in Wuhan dropping in the streets like flies. Leaked video from China....hmmm...doubtful. Never happened anywhere else. Stoke fear. Stoke Confusion. Stoke panic.

Television......Tell-A-Vision......Tell-A-Story......Tell-A-Lie

CNN death count tally in real time. Is that even possible? Doesn't matter, they'll believe it. Create panic. Create fear. Erase critical thought. Manipulate.

Television......Tell-A-Vision......Tell-A-Story......Tell-A-Lie

Testing, tracking, tracing. **Where's the flu?** False positives abound. That's ok, log it in. Change "dying with" to "dying from". Jack up the numbers. Fear fuels the narrative. Ban early treatment. Ban Ivermectin. Vent and Remdesivir to increase mortality. Are they scared? Hell yes, they're scared. Good, it keeps them in line.

Television......Tell-A-Vision......Tell-A-Story......Tell-A-Lie

Lock them down. Close their businesses. Isolate. Tell them what to feel. Tell them what to think. Control their reaction. Strip their freedoms. They won't complain. They're too afraid. Not enough. Masks will symbolize submission. Dangle freedom like a carrot on a stick. Make the jab optional...at first. Not enough compliance. Make it mandatory. Turn them against each other. They're easier to control when divided.

Television......Tell-A-Vision......Tell-A-Story......Tell-A-Lie

Jabs are causing autoimmune disease, blood clots, strokes, and heart attacks. Killing many. Narrative is crumbling. Quick! End the story. Claim success because of mandates and freedom limitations, that leaves the door open to do it again. And we will do it again. And they will surrender again. Fear motivates. Lather. Rinse. Repeat.

Television......Tell-A-Vision......Tell-A-Story......Tell-A-Lie

Switch to climate change. We're all gonna' die! They'll forgo, we'll build our mansions. On coastal properties, nonetheless. So much for rising sea levels. And green energy, sshhh...don't tell them that's supplied through child and slave labor.

Television......Tell-a-Vision......Tell-A-Story......Tell-A-Lie

Ukraine. Hide the truth. Puppets installed. Clinton foundation. Money laundering. Child trafficking. Organ trafficking. Laptop. Bio-labs. Keep attention away from corruption, failed policies, CDC fraud and Pfizer documents. Soooo many side effects. Where's Fauci? All the world's a stage. When eyes are deceived, minds are deceived.

Television......Tell-A-Vision......Tell-A-Story......Tell-A-Lie

George Soros, Klaus Schwab. Monsters behind the curtain. World Economic Forum. The New World Order. The Great Reset underway. You will own nothing and be happy. You will be enslaved to them. One world government. Complete surveillance state. Digital currency. Transhumanism. Social credit score determines if you eat.

This is the world the Leftists are ushering in for you and your children. Speak up, while you still have a voice. Vote them out, while you still have a choice.

Television......now it's time to Tell-The-Truth

THE CHOKEHOLD

Will you take our hand voluntarily?
No, you don't want it?
You don't want our help?
That doesn't really matter
We gave you the illusion of choice
We'll use just one finger to hold you steady
Place one finger around your throat
It's just for two weeks, then we promise we'll let go
You're caught in a chokehold and you don't even realize
You're so bamboozled you think we're the good guys
Two weeks have come and gone
We said we'd let go, **but that was a lie**
We need to put one more finger around your throat
We need to hold on to keep you in place
It's best to stay away from others
Solitude equals safety
You're fine without your family, you're fine without your friends
Your mental health can and will be sacrificed
Here's a mask to remind you that you belong to us
To remind you whose orders you follow
To remind you that you must play the game
Is our grip feeling tighter?
A little, you say, but not enough to complain
It's for your own good, remember?
Now's a good time to slip three fingers around your throat
So quickly you didn't see it coming
You're caught in a chokehold and you don't even realize
You're so bamboozled you think we're the good guys
You can't go to work now
Close your business, it's ok we'll take care of you
Just give us some time to get these checks out
How much clearer can we make it, **you are not a priority**
What's that? You can't feed your children now?
Sorry, we can't relate

We're using one hand to feed ourselves while the other holds you in place

Can you breathe? Can you? We see you're fighting for air

Oops, you're slipping

It's time to add a fourth finger

Four fingers around your throat

You want us to let go a little bit, just enough so you can breathe?

We can do that as long as you do something for us

Get this shot, then we'll loosen our grip

And more down the line at our discretion

Not just for you, but for your children as well

They need to learn to follow orders, too

You're caught in a chokehold and you don't even realize

You're so bamboozled you think we're the good guys

Don't bother reaching for that gun

It's not there

Remember, we took it away

We took it for your safety

It's better this way

Our grip remains firm when you have no defense

It's time we add the final finger

Slow and steady was the plan

One....finger....at....a....time

Now five fingers around your throat

We'll convince your children they are confused, expose them to pornography

Groom.... groom.... groom

Teach them to hate you, their country, and to turn away from God

Compliance led you into subjugation

And your kids will pay the price

They will never know what true freedom is

They stand behind you, in the line you fell into

And those not yet, because of you, will be born **with our fingers around their throat**

Your silence was our success

You're caught in a chokehold and you don't even realize

You're so bamboozled you think we're the good guys

THE CROOKED COUNTY COUNCILMAN

Hello, and welcome to tonight's episode of "The Crooked County Councilman," staring our very own Sam Page and brought to you in part by Pfizer: "Just because we've paid out more than $4.7 BILLION in fines over the past 20 years for 80 different crimes and violations doesn't mean you can't trust us, right?...............right?"

Sam, you are going around telling your partners in crime in the media that we here at the council meetings are spreading misinformation. **THAT IS A LIE**! The medical information that has been shared at these meetings is evidence based, backed by peer reviewed scientific journals, and corroborated by thousands of doctors and healthcare workers worldwide. Your only talking point is the robotic mantra "safe and effective, safe and effective." A phrase meant to induce mass compliance through psychological manipulation solidified in the world of "if you repeat a lie often enough it becomes the truth."

What data have you presented to refute our information? ZERO! You do not have any because we are presenting facts.

You stand on your self ordained pedestal and shout **"misinformation,"** but you have nothing to back it up.

Show us your data, Sam. Prove to us that myocarditis, blood clots, strokes, heart attacks, miscarriages, paralysis, and death are **not** occuring from these shots. You can't because it **is happening** in astronomical numbers. See, at this point it is no longer up to us to prove serious and deadly adverse events are happening. It is up to **you** to prove they are **not**.

How about we read some information directly from Pfizer:
"Myocarditis and pericarditis have occurred in some people who have received the vaccine."
"Serious and unexpected side effects may occur. The possible side effects of the vaccine are **still being studied in clinical trials."**

Or from Moderna:
"Myocarditis and pericarditis have occurred in some people who have received the Moderna COVID-19 vaccine."
"Serious and unexpected side effects may occur. The Moderna COVID -19 Vaccine **is still being studied in clinical trials."**

According to The Mayo Clinic, observational data show 5- year survival rates that approximate 50% for those with verified myocarditis. That means when diagnosed with myocarditis you have about a 50/50 chance of still being alive after 5 years. The facts may be uncomfortable, Sam, but they're something people should be aware of before they consent to this injection for themselves and/or their children.

And finally, this gem from J and J: "The reporting rate of thrombosis with thrombocytopenia following the administration of the Janssen COVID -19 Vaccine has been highest in females ages 18 through 49 years; **some cases have been fatal."** Translation: they died, Sam

Is this all "misinformation"? Perhaps you'd like to personally write to or call out the scientists of the Moderna, Pfizer, and J and J trials who authored the injection fact sheets? Oh, but that would be biting the hand that feeds you, wouldn't it?

Your intentional omission of adverse events constitutes **DISINFORMATION** and the consequences therefrom can be detrimental to the health and wellbeing of adults and children. I find it disgusting that you call a product "safe" when it can cause serious injury and death and "effective" when it doesn't stop infection or transmission.

FIRST DO NO HARM, SAM. Remember that? INFORMED CONSENT..... does that not matter to you?
You need to grow a pair, man up, develop a moral backbone and start discussing the very real present and future dangers possible with these shots.

THE DATING GAME: MARXIST EDITION

From the County Council, the corruption capital of St. Louis, it's The Dating Game, Marxist Edition. I'm your host, Kim Landgraf, now let's meet our three eligible communists, I mean bachelorettes:

Bachelorette Number One is a young lady who enjoys dropping the F bomb on social media, encourages children to read pornography, has more boosters than frequent flyer miles and can be quoted as saying, "Duh, it's not a baby until it's born" please say hello to she/her Calisa Fancy!

Bachelorette Number Two is a young lady who interchanges Dr. Seuss with the Bible and loves coal powered green energy. Say hello to Shelli Funnaway!
"Hey, y'all! I'd like to give a quick shout out to my homegirl AOC! **Climate change is real girl!**"

And Bachelorette Number Three, a young lady who keeps a voice recording of herself just so she can hear herself talk and believes freedoms are just some words on a wrinkly old piece of paper. Say hello to Walonda Shebb!

And now let's introduce our bachelor: He's been known to hold two jobs at once, is the founder and CEO of the Keep Your Hands Clean And Under The Table Consulting Firm, owns stock in a padlock company, absolutely hates whistleblowers and has a Pfizer tattoo right across his forehead, please welcome Scam Wage.

"Good evening comrades. Bachelorette Number Three, I absolutely abhor the Constitution, please tell me in your own words what you hate about it."

"It's all those pesky little phrases like, **SHALL NOT BE INFRINGED, ABRIDGING THE FREEDOM OF SPEECH, TO BE SECURE IN THEIR PERSONS, WE THE PEOPLE, BLAH, BLAH, BLAH.** I mean if people were actually paying attention they'd realize I'm breaking my oath to it, so...yeah...it's a pain in the butt."

"Bachelorette Number One, same question."

"The Consti what??"

"Hmmm......Ok, I like that answer!"

"Bachelorette Number Two, If I choose you and happen to come into a lot of money, would you have a problem with how I spend it?"

"Oh, I don't care, Scammy. I'm just a mouthpiece. You do what you like and I'll defend you in a long, drawn out, emotion packed tirade."

"Bachelorette Number one, same question."

"Well, as long as you set up a fund for Planned Homicide, I mean Parenthood, you can get away with, I mean, spend it how you like."

"Number Three?"

"Hmmm......you can spend it how you like as long as I can force people to decide between a medical intervention of my choosing or feeding their families."

Well, Scam, the ladies have given you a lot to think about. Will it be Commie Number One, Commie Number Two, or Commie Number Three?

"Actually, Kim, I've decided to choose all three! Many hands lighten the load as they say."

Hold on, Bachelorette Number One, come back! You can't go stomping out in the middle of the show!

"Oh, yes, I can! I'm the best. I'm the smartest. Why didn't Scam choose just me? **I'm the pretty princess!**"

That doesn't matter, Calisa, we say jump and you say how high.

Now let's see where you four sympathizers will be heading to for a date!

Pack your bags, you're all headed for the Grand Gulag, located on the shores of the Yellow Sea in a small coastal village in North Korea.
And guess what? Since you've spent your careers stripping away the God-given rights of others, you'll be happy to know your stay at The Grand Gulag **will be permanent!**

You'll be spending your days and nights working your fingers to the bone, silenced by the state and wishing you would have appreciated the freedoms outlined and safeguarded for you in the U.S. Constitution.

Well, that's it for tonight's edition of The Dating Game Marxist Edition. Good night and remember, you will own nothing and be happy, at least that's what we'll tell you!

THE DEMOCRATIC ABYSS

It's been two long years throughout which
Democrats have ignored the true science
They are more concerned with virtue signaling
Than using critical thought for reliance

And the injection they mandated
In one corrupt breath
How do they sleep at night knowing
One side effect is death?

Miss Clancy, decreeing orders from your illusory throne
Critical thought is not your style
I'd bet a peak of your cell phone shows
The health department on speed dial

Doing what you are told
Though your party's a sinking ship
Anyone with such blind obedience to authority
Has no business in leadership

The way you speak to your fellow councilmembers
Often times condescending and rude
We sit here and bare witness to
The self-righteousness that's imbued

Tim being drawn out through redistricting
Has clear malicious intent
I can almost hear the Soros funded Democrats say
Now that was money well spent!

More Democrats in power
Is a nightmare for everyone
If they continue uninterrupted
Sadly, America will be done

Obama signed HR 4310 into law
Allowing propaganda to be used on the U.S. population
That laid the groundwork for the Mainstream Media
To spread their self-serving lies throughout the nation

Today's mainstream journalists swim in a cesspool of corruption
From truth they've made their descent
They are nothing more than obedient lapdogs
For the corporations they represent

They use CGI technology and recycled photos
To manipulate and to deceive
What you witness with your eyes
You can no longer trust or believe

Their goal is to manipulate public thought
For whatever agenda they want to advance
Pushing the globalists' aim of a New World Order
For centralized control of the world's finance

The media's silence on elite pedophiles
Is deafening to the ears
Protect your kids from the government and Hollywood
They've been grooming our children for years

Gates and China buying up farmland
Should serve to rouse your suspicion
Their ultimate endgame to gain control
Is to starve you into submission

There's more to the Ukraine than many understand
Money-laundering, child trafficking, bioweapons, and laptop
If the politicians lose their connections there
The billions lining their pockets will stop

They ignore Canada, Australia, and New Zealand
As peaceful protesters are beat to the ground
Clearly their political agenda decides
Which countries' cries for freedom are drowned

Mainstream news' only purpose
Is to control public reaction
Rule of thumb, if the media covers it
It's a lie serving as a distraction

Your best chance at hearing the truth
Is to turn off the corporate run news
Seek out independent journalists
Whose paychecks don't dictate their views

Look to the World Economic Forum
To understand the evil at our door
Schwab and Soros are the monsters
Leading nations into war

Liberals demonize patriotism
And remove God from the equation
All attempts at retaining our liberties
Are met with vehement dissuasion

We must not get comfortable
And we must not forget
To our freedoms the Left
Will always pose a threat

The Constitution was crafted for We The People
And indeed it is us who hold the power
It is our responsibility to retain our liberties
And never in the face of tyranny to cower

For every freedom you surrender
And every time your voice you quell
Only serves in adding another bar
To your very own prison cell

THE END OF THE WORLD AS WE KNOW IT

That sucked!! It started with a lockdown
Birx and Fauci, a zoom call
And many people were very afraid

Lies from the politicians, rights under their conditions
World fears its own kind, don't gather with your own kind
Slow it down a notch, isolate, hide, no sense
The CDC chatters decide what matters, push fear of germs, more germs
Test at **behest**, slaves to the system
In a government **obsessed** with their own terms
To hospitals to die, they're sent
With a vent shoved down.... their.... neck

Lie after lie reported, confusion, fear, mask up
Ban meds that save lives! Fine, then
Uh, oh, don't ya know, depopulate, greater good
It's what to do. Save yourself, hide yourself
Amazon serves your **needs,** watch the middle class **bleed**
Close stores, close churches, dialogs raise questions; smite, smite
The Left, unpatriotic, loot, fight, ignite cities in bright light
Feeling anything but contrite

It's the end of the world as we know it
It's the end of the world as we know it
It's the end of the world as we know it, and I don't feel fine

CNN Propaganda hour
Soros is a global power
Lie and articulate, manipulate
Common sense will abate
Fall in line and keep on lock-step walking, conforming
Politicians two-faced. Socialism interlaced
Close the schools, close the minds
Dumb down, dumb down
Watch your mouth, hush, hush
Uh oh, this means mandate, clots await

Shots affect the birth rate
A booster, a booster
A booster is a scam
There were solutions, there were alternatives
But they were de....nied

It's the end of the world as we know it
It's the end of the world as we know it
The kids suffered from their time alone
It's the end of the world as we know it, and I don't feel fine

Schools filled with pornography
Families drift di-vide
Pedophelia normalized
Epstein Island, Epstein flight logs
Bill Gates, Klaus Schwab
Green New Deal, Reset, Social score, WEF!
End servitude, be patriotic, fight; for your kids, right? (RIGHT!)

It's the end of the world as we know it
It's the end of the world as we know it
The kids suffered from their time alone
It's the end of the world as we know it, and I don't feel fine
The kids suffered from their time alone
And things are not fine

THE GATES OF HEAVEN

I don't pretend to know what's at the gates of Heaven or what judgment awaits me there.
I only know the deeds I've done and the things I've asked in prayer

At times I've asked for abundance, placed too much value on wealth
Not appreciating the day to day and the simple joy that comes with good health

I've fought with my family, over many things inconsequential
Sometimes forgetting that it is our love that remains essential

I've tried to advocate for the unborn, to give voice to God's creation
Hoping to touch the hearts of those advocating for their assassination

I try to remain humble with the Holy Spirit as my guide
And refrain from committing transgressions under the guise of pride

I've fallen short on kindness on more than one occasion
Sometimes forgetting that selflessness is a big part of the equation

I hope the times I've done what's right
By far outnumber the times I'd lost sight

I hope I gave comfort every chance I was able
And shared food and drink from the bounties of my table

And when I led with my head thinking I was being smart
Jesus, please forgive me when those times broke your heart

I pray you wait for me at the gates as I navigate through my imperfection
And welcome me with open arms and the strength of your protection

For the only way to the Father is through you
Jesus, please guide me in all that I do

THE K.E.L.L.I. INSTITUTE

Common sense and rational thought, qualities that we as conservatives take for granted in the sense that we mistakenly like to assume these traits are possessed by all. Sadly, it is becoming more and more evident with each passing year that this is far from the case. So, in an effort to alter the upward trajectory of the mental disorder that is Liberalism, I have taken it upon myself to found an establishment whose mission is to gently heal and de-program those on the Left; with the hope of one day turning them into productive members of society. During the course of a year-long program, I and my team of common sense advocates will **Kindly Eradicate Leftists Liberal Indoctrination. The K.E.L.L.I. Institute of Neuroregenerative Repair** stands ever firm in its commitment to put an end to the cult-like ideology being force fed to so many in our community.

Don't know the difference between a man and a woman? No problem, we'll explain it to you!

Still eating that vegan biscotti and drinking that soy milk latte? We'll introduce you to the joys of a good ole' fashioned cup of Joe and a nice juicy ribeye.

Not sure how to handle that swelling call to violence when you hear an opposing view? We'll give you the tools you need to implement rational thought.

Part of our **"return to sanity"** program here at the **K.E.L.L.I. Institute** includes three books on the required reading list:

1. *The Liberal Mind: Where Hate and Mental Instability Go to Party*
2. *Not Every Space is a Safe Space, That's What a Backbone is For* and
3. *How to Escape the Hive and Reclaim Your Intellect*

Courses at **The K.E.L.L.I. Institute** include:

- XX, XY, Biology Don't Lie
- Waking Up From Woke
- Reality Check: The Globalists Hate You
  and
- Understanding *The View*: When Psychosis Manifests Itself as a Talk Show

Patients, I mean, guests, will also have a weekly obligatory session in the "**Truth Booth**" where they will be exposed to a variety of cold hard facts crucial to reclaiming sensibility. Facts such as:

- Real men don't wear skinny jeans
- Rainbow colored hair is **not** attractive
- Coal, oil, and natural gas power electricity
  and
- There are no Starbucks in a communist society

Social activities will be held in Freedom Hall and include our ever popular game of **"Pin the Kid on the EV"** where guests are blindfolded and attempt to tack the photo of a lithium-mining third world country child onto a photo of a Tesla.

There will also be 24/7 live stream coverage of illegals flooding the U.S./Mexico border and guests are encouraged to watch clips from the **"summer of love"** as churches, businesses, and police stations were vandalized and burned down by MAGA conservatives...oh, wait, I'm sorry, it was the Soros backed Leftists who did that! There will also be real time footage of birds being slaughtered by wind turbines.

The end of year graduation ceremony will include the mandatory tasks of reciting the phrase, "Yikes, I've been duped! It's a muzzle, not a mask!", scraping the I Love Dr. Fauci bumper sticker off your Prius and replacing it with the more appropriate LET'S GO BRANDON decal, and singing the **K.E.L.L.I. Institute alma mater:**

I was once a naive Liberal
Living in the dark
Relying on the mainstream media narrative
As a moral benchmark

I hereby promise I will enact my brain
To be objectively observative
Hurray! I have finally seen the light
I'm now a proud conservative!

THE LAST TWO YEARS

The last two years have been eye opening for all
The Democrats have really shown their stripes
Crime's exploding, Constitution's suspended
But, hey, at least they're providing free crack pipes!

The Biden administration aims
To keep your health on track
Be sure to pull your mask back up
When you're done smoking crack!

Democrats bare faced when mingling with the public
Should make your indignation more fervent
You must wear a mask, not them
Because to them **you** are the servant

They place little value on character and achievement
Being gained by individual accord
How much do you want to bet it was a Democrat
Who invented the participation award?

They impose tyranny
And obliterate freedom of choice
Do they feel proud when they explain to their kids
"It was I who stole your voice?"

Democrats regard freedoms as privileges
But, here's something to jolt them awake
We get our freedoms from God
They were **never** theirs to take

Praising politicians for lifting restrictions
And letting you earn your dough
Is like thanking your kidnappers
For finally letting you go

The Left are the most intolerant of all
And use censorship to exert their dominion
Sure, we'll listen to you, they say
As long as you share our opinion

Our southern border is wide open
And the Left don't seem to care
You'd think they'd have more compassion
For the children being trafficked there

But what can you expect from those
Who sacrifice children for the greater good?
And everyday murdering babies
By supporting Planned Parenthood

To the environment, the Left claim
Such care and devotion
I wonder how many of their non-biodegradable masks
Will end up in the ocean?

And politicians flying into Davos
In their own personal jets
I guess carbon emissions don't count
If you've got the right assets

Democrats feel threatened
By the critically thinking majority
They don't like dealing with those who question
Blind obedience to authority

To all of you proudly carrying your vax pass
And doing what you are told
At what point were you ok with
Becoming a QR code?

Interesting some blue states are dropping their mandates
Seems now they're ok with germs
I'm **almost absolutely certain** it has nothing to do with
Their polling numbers for the midterms

Forcing a mask, a lockdown, and an injection
Are all in violation of the Constitution
And, no, "I was just following orders"
Will not exempt you from prosecution

When the dust finally settles and all truths are revealed
Though it may seem insurmountable
All those complicit in unconstitutional acts
Will be held accountable

THE LEFTIST PLAYBOOK

We can't have control, if they have control
And that's just not in the cards
We are your government and we're here to help
From birth to the graveyards

Minimize parental influence
Nanny state sponsored Early Childhood Education is the key
Sexualize the children
The trusted teacher becomes the predator
The trusted teacher is the groomer
Use semantics to legitimize perversion
Interchange "pedophile" with "Minor Attracted Person"

Falsify history with CRT
Drill it into their heads
Teach them skin color is everything
You are born a racist, you are born a victim
Demasculinize, defeminize, de-identify
Tell them what to think
Tell them what to feel
Educate them just enough to be a beneficial cog in the machine but, not enough to remove us
Devalue human life by killing the most innocent among us:
The unborn child

Remove the father from the equation
Destroy the family unit
Two jobs to keep food on the table
Tax them into oblivion
Then launder that money back to us
No quality time, only survival
Stressful life is a painful life
Hook them on pharmaceuticals

Use the media to spread our lies

Convince the people the truth is not what you see with your eyes, it's what we tell your eyes to see
Erase all natural instinct
Make them dependent
If they'll hurt each other over a toilet paper shortage, imagine what they'll do to each other over a food shortage
Depopulate, depopulate
Global cooling....no....global warming....no....global cooling....no....global warming
Whatever makes them more afraid
Most of them are useless eaters anyway

We can't have control, if they have control
And that's just not in the cards
We are your government and we're here to help
From birth to the graveyards

Eradicate small family farms
Self-sustainability is a threat to the agenda
Bugs are filled with parasites, let them eat them to their detriment
More illness equals more profit for pharma funneled back to us
All three letter agencies to be corporate captured
Central Bank Digital Currency is a valuable step towards enslavement
They will own nothing and WE will be happy

Point a finger before a finger is pointed at us
The proles must never know there was no 'big switch'
We are EXACTLY our grandfather's party
Pander and virtue signal relentlessly
Conceal the fact that the Democratic Party is the true threat to this nation
Image is everything, truth is nothing
Establish a cult like mentality to materialize our inciteful rhetoric against those who oppose

NEVER discuss increasing homelessness, the empty bellies of American children, or the chaos, destruction, violence, and murder committed by the Left

NEVER let the media show the children's underwear hanging from rape trees near the border

No voter ID
Get those illegal aliens to the poles!
Then send them down south to pick crops
Slips of the tongue reveal our true character
So he sniffs and gropes children and took showers with his young daughter
Ten percent for the big guy and the rest for crack cocaine and prostitutes for the son
Come on, man. No joke
Dead people casting ballots worked in 2020, but will it work again?
Cheat, lie, cheat, lie, cheat, lie, repeat

We can't have control, if they have control
And that's just not in the cards
We are your government and we're here to help
From birth to the graveyards

THE ROOM NEXT DOOR

So much can happen in the room next door
The room next door, the room next door
So much can happen in the room next door
Especially if you're on the ninth floor

Corruption follows the Democrats
Like a gossling does the goose
If they're not doing it for the money
It's their ignorance on the loose

Sam can sure really pick 'em
His amoral administration doesn't fool us
Let's at least hope the ninth floor janitor
Got a recompensable cleaning bonus

Ah, but what's a sex scandal or two
When you're a Liberal politician
If all their deeds were taped
Surely they'd all be in prison

So much can happen in the room next door
The room next door, the room next door
So much can happen in the room next door
Especially if you're on the ninth floor

What really happens in and around Sam's office?
Oh, what you could hear as a fly upon those walls!
Tick tock 'till all truths are revealed
Democrats hands are dirtier than public bathroom stalls

Siphoning money from here to there
Who really knows where it's all going
Interesting how many Democrats'
Bank accounts are overflowing

Ladies, you may want to rethink your submission to Sam
If you want your freedom to prevail
And start asking yourself, hey, is it worth it?
And can I later afford my bail?

So much can happen in the room next door
The room next door, the room next door
So much can happen in the room next door
Especially if you're on the ninth floor

So much corruption lies within those walls
So many people hurt along the way
Innumerable businesses and lives devastated
Because they didn't want to pay to play

Trampling on our God-given freedoms
Laying waste to the Constitution
Tightening the grip around our throats
With every resolution

As more truths come to light
And sweet justice leads the way
The only place we want to see Sam is dressed in orange
Picking up trash along the highway

So much can happen in the room next door
The room next door, the room next door
So much can happen in the room next door
Especially if you're on the ninth floor

THE SCAM

Two weeks to flatten the curve
Is how this all began
Of course that was the cover for the beginning of
A much more nefarious plan

The PCR tests fueled this scam
They weren't meant for viral detection
When they run the cycles high enough
Everyone has an infection

The test swabs are sterilized with Ethylene Oxide, a known carcinogen
The test solution contains Sodium Azide
Hopefully, they're too dumb to realize! they say
Keep filling their water with fluoride!

The CDC is a company
That makes money off what they recommend
They own many vaccine patents
And are glad to call pharma their friend

The protocols are killing people
It is death by selection
So many lives have perished
By withholding Ivermectin

People mask up in fear, then are angry with those
Who haven't fallen for the same mass hypnosis
Their reaction has nothing to do with societal health
And everything to do with mass psychosis

Able minded doctors know these masks are a ruse
And don't stop viral transmission
Not knowing this makes them either illiterate or incompetent
And one heck of a lousy clinician

Adults sacrificing children to make **themselves** feel safe
Stealing kids' formative years
Inside that mask they suffocate them in
Hides a reservoir of tears

We look around and it doesn't make sense
We're patronized if we ask why
If what they're telling us now isn't the truth
How much of history is a lie?

The jabs are not faring
Quite how they were expected
It's interesting the one's getting sick
Are mainly the one's injected

The shots wreak havoc
And compromise your health
And with pharma's zero liability
They add billions to their wealth

Stop believing all the lies
It's not a breakthrough case
It simply means the product
Has fallen on its face

Jabs cause viruses to mutate
You can research it, it's a fact
But your not supposed to know that
Imagine all the indignation that would attract

Vaccine Acquired Immune Deficiency Syndrome
Is what happens in the repeatedly injected
It means the shots are eroding their immune system
And they will never be protected

Someone get Sam a tissue
As his narrative is falling apart
Recommending a failed product
Is not really very smart

Putting kids in danger
With the policies of the Left
I've never seen a man
So morally bereft

Quick! Remask the public! decrees Sam
Refuel the propaganda and fear!
Those darn critical thinkers are ruining
My hopes for a vaccine passport this year

The ladies on this council seem to vote
How Sam says they can
They claim to be strong, independent women
Yet take their orders from a man

Ladies, staying obedient to Sam
Is both very sad and odd
You've now proven you're nothing more than
Members of the Page Pep Squad

The Left push mandates
And fill your life with strife
They want less freedom for you
And a lower quality of life

Dependence on the government
Is their all encompassing goal
Because when you are dependent
You **are** no longer whole

The only way the day will come
When this BS will no longer apply
Is when everyone starts **thinking again**
And we all no longer comply

For tyranny only survives
If the people give it breath
Only without the inhalation of our surrender
Will it die it's deserved death

THE YOUNG AND THE CLUELESS- episode 1

Good evening and welcome to tonight's episode of *The Young and the Clueless* starring Calisa Fancy as the young bright eyed gullible Leftist ever too willing to bow to authority, Shelli Funnaway as the EV loving climate change connoisseur who desperately wishes **she** had authored the Green New Deal, Walonda Shebb, the anti Constitutionalist, ever ready to strip away our God given rights of free speech, defense, and medical autonomy and Scam Wage, a man so busy living in and taking from the pockets of others, he's completely lost his moral compass.

Tonight's episode begins with Scam standing in an office (anywhere but a hospital, wink...wink) as Walonda bursts through the door. "Scam!" she says, "I've got great news! I've organized a **Surrender Your Guns to Help Liberate a Country** gun control rally! Every law-abiding U.S. citizen is encouraged to donate **their** firearms to help citizens in **other** nations defend themselves from their respective country's oppressive regime. Scam, are you even listening to me? What are you doing? Why did you grab that broom?"

"Of course, I'm listening, Walonda, it's just I've got **so many things** I need to sweep under the rug here, it literally takes up the majority of my time. A gun control rally? That's a great idea! I would tag along, but my armed bodyguard has the day off today."

Suddenly there's a knock at the door. **"Come in if you're not MAGA!"** shout Scam and Walonda.

It's Shelli and she enters the room beaming from ear to ear holding up a picture of a young boy.
"Guess what, guy and gal! Oops, sorry, I didn't mean to assume gender. Guess what, comrades? I'm so proud of myself! This is a picture of Bongolo, a young boy from the Democratic Republic of the Congo whom I've begun to sponsor. He and his family are working so hard to mine the lithium I need for my EV battery and I figure since working in the mines lowers his life expectancy considerably, I can sponsor a new child every year! It feels so good to be a humanitarian!"

Just then, there's another knock at the door. **"Come in if you're not MAGA!"** shout Scam, Walonda, and Shelli.

Calisa enters with a relieved expression on her face (at least we think so as she is wearing a mask). "Oh, thank Marx you're still here, Walonda. I was worried you'd left for the gun control rally without me! Remember, though, the pro-abortion rally begins right before the gun control rally and I definitely want to attend that! Advocating for killing children **in** the womb is just as important to me as protecting children **outside** the womb."

"Of course I waited for you, Calisa!" replies Walonda, "but why are you still wearing that mask? It's been over two years now since I've seen your face!"

"Oh," replies Calisa, "I had this mask surgically attached. You'll never see **my** face again! **We will NEVER be safe!"** insists Calisa emphatically, **"MASKS SAVE LIVES!!"**

"Actually, Calisa, before you go" interjects Scam, "I'd like to talk to you alone for a minute concerning that blistering rash on your arm."

"No, Scam," answers Calisa, "when you speak to one of us, you speak to all of us! You should know by now we are incapable of forming our own opinions!"

"You're right, how could I forget. Group think mentality is the lifeline of progressive politics."
I'm just concerned, I mean, I used to practice medicine, (wink, wink) and I've seen that rash in pictures before......"

"Oh, no!" exclaim Shelli and Walonda in unison.
"You don't think......it couldn't be......we hope it's not......MONKEY POX!!

DUNN......DUNN......DUNN......DUNN

THE YOUNG AND THE CLUELESS- episode 2

Tonight's episode of **The Young and the Clueless** finds us outside an Anti-Ultra MAGA Rally organized by Calisa Fancy and Shelli Funnaway. Calisa and Shelli have set up a T-shirt booth just in front of the rally in the hopes of selling their "My Body, My Choice, Unless the CDC Recommends Otherwise" shirts.

"Oh, Shelli, thank you again for not celebrating Columbus Day with me. It's good friends like you who truly understand that when I say I support the indigenous population I'm only talking about here in the U.S. You and I both know that the rights of indigenous populations in third world countries must be sacrificed in the name of science. If it wasn't for the genocidal maniac, pseudo philanthropist Bill Gates and his unethical experiments on babies, children, women, and men in countries like India and Africa, we would never know the lethality of vaccines and how to best cover-up their terrible side effects before they reach the world market. I mean, they have to test them on **SOMEBODY** first. It's so courageous of the poor to take one for the team!"

"What was that, Calisa?" asked Shelli. "Sorry, I was just reading through my Official AOC Fan Girl Membership Manual. **AOC is a genius.** She made such a statement with Tax the Rich stretched across her booty in that custom made designer dress."

Out of the corner of her eye, Calisa spots Walonda Shebb hiding behind a tree near their stand.

"Shalonda! What are you doing? Why are you hiding?"

"SHHHH, Calisa! Quiet! I was just coming to check on you girls, but I can't be seen!"

"Why not?" inquired Calisa and Shelli together.

"Well, I keep reading about all of these people, especially young, otherwise healthy men, who are dropping dead from heart attacks and blood clots relating to the Covid shot. I mandated that thing for county employees, remember? I refused to research or read through the Pfizer data and instead let politics and payouts take precedence over common sense and bodily autonomy. I mean how long can **"ignorance is bliss"** cover for the truth of **"ignorance is a choice?"**

"It's been working for us so far!" replied Shelli and Calisa in unison.

Just then a nice looking fellow in a MAGA cap approached their stand.

"Shelli!" cried Calisa, "Call whatever police department we didn't defund! This guy is probably dangerous!"

"Well, hello, ladies," began the nice looking fellow in the MAGA cap, "I was just wondering what your rally is all about. I see it's sponsored by the 'Woke American Communist Crusade Organization'. You do realize its acronym is WACCO, right?"

"Listen Ultra MAGA man," answers Calisa. "I **need** the government to tell me what to think and how to react. As Kamala Harris would say, 'Freedom is offensive because it is offensive to some, therefore it must be offensive to all because without some we do not have all and without all we will never have the some of our parts.' I watched her say that on CNN, so it's the truth."

"I, of course, will be in the political class once the Soros funded color revolution goes into full effect," continued Calisa, "I feel it is my duty as a college educated white liberal to speak on behalf of those I deem oppressed."

"You do know that this communist utopia you envision has you forfeiting your personal property, getting microchipped, 24/7 surveillance and eating bugs?" The nice looking fellow retorted.

"Yes," Shelli snapped back, "but, we will all get **equal** amounts of bugs, **duh!**"

Just then Scam Wage went zooming by on a bicycle.

"Hold up! Come join us!" Calisa shouted after Scam. "You hate MAGA, too!"

"Sorry, girls, I can't stop!" yelled Scam. "This Mantovani guy is on my tail!"

"He's already passed me up a few times and it looks like he's going to win this race!"

"Oh, no!" exclaimed Shelli and Calisa in exasperation. "If Scam loses and Mantovani wins, you know what that means?"

DUN DUN DUN DUN........

"ACCOUNTABILITY!!!"

THEN THEY CAME FOR MY VOICE

Then they came for my voice
Just don't say that they said
It's best to keep the peace
But it's important, how do I let them know?
What does it pertain to? **It pertains to me.** Well who are you? **I am but one person, but part of a larger whole**
Stop rocking the boat
We don't like what you say. You're a nuisance, you're making waves, you're ruining it for others, **they shouted as they came for my voice.**
But if I lose my voice, yours will soon follow
My voice is your voice, I struggled to say
So, I sat and I watched as injustices were done. I sat and I watched as events unfolded, as intensity increased **as even the ones who desired my silence now struggled to speak**
And I sat there with thoughts running through my mind
I tried! I tried! I tried! These two words desperately trying to find passage
I reached to remove the binding that surely must be wrapped 'round my mouth, but there was nothing there **and yet still I could not utter a word**
And I looked out mournfully from the jagged shore at so many floating in a sea of voluntary complacency, wearing the comfort of social acceptance like a life vest
Then strength from above filled my lungs, as I finally cried out
My voice is your voice
And I will stand for you as I stand for myself
United in the understanding **that when they strike the words from our lips, they render us inconsequential**
It's just a matter of time
I am but a scapegoat
They will come for your voice
And the silence will be deafening
As we're thrown back in time
When inequality stained the fabric of our humanity

106

When rights and liberties for some were decided by the few
And those who stood up and brought discomfort knew **that it is in discomfort that progress is made**
It is in discomfort that voices are heard, that policies are implemented and changed, and that people can be free
And our children, what will they know?
For they stand behind us in the line we fall into
And I looked around as my life was being decided for me
And I spoke up
Then they came for my voice

Thump-thump......thump-thump

Hi, mommy! It's been four weeks now and my heart is beating really fast, between 105 and 121 times per minute!

Thump-thump......thump-thump

Just one week later and my brain, back bone, spinal cord, lungs and heart are all developing! I am growing, mommy! I'm going to be so big and strong for you! I can't hear you yet, but I'm so excited to meet you!

Thump-thump......thump-thump

Six weeks and my arms and legs are forming! I bet I'll be a great soccer player!

Thump-thump......thump-thump

Seven weeks! Man, how time flies! My brain and my face are rapidly developing along with my eyelids, bones, nostrils, and retinas! I bet you smell great, mommy!

Thump-thump......thump-thump

Eight weeks! This is an important milestone for me! All my major organs are formed and growing along with the tube connecting my throat and lungs so I can let out a nice cry when we first meet!

Thump-thump......thump-thump

Nine weeks now and my nose and facial features are more prominent! I hope I look like you, mommy! Even though I can't see you yet, I just know that you are beautiful!

Thump-thump......thump-thump

I've been so busy growing and I think I'm about twelve weeks old now! My head is rounding out, my eyelids and ears continue to develop. I've got big, strong muscles forming and my liver is even producing red blood cells! I'm moving around in here, but you probably can't feel it yet!

Thump-thump......thump-thump

Fourteen weeks, here I am! My sex hormones are being produced, I can even pee! All my organs are fully formed and growing steadily. I can move my hands to my mouth. So that's what my thumb is for! Soon I'll be able to taste and smell!

Thump-thump......thump-thump

Sixteen weeks! I can roll and flip! Did you feel me, mommy? That little kick was to say hello! My heart is pumping up to 100 pints of blood every day and my hair follicles are starting to develop. I sure hope my hair is brown like yours!. My digestive system is working and I can now hear sounds! That means I can hear your voice, mommy, and that makes me so happy!

Thump-thump......thump-thump

We went somewhere today and you talked to another lady. Were you talking about me? Were you telling her all about me? Will she be our new friend? She said for us to come back in a few days, so I guess she's our friend.

Thump-thump......thump-thump

We're back to see that lady again. This time there's even more people here. I wonder why they gave you that dress to wear? Are we taking a nap, is that why you're lying down? Are you still awake, mommy? I can't hear you anymore, but I hear other people talking and other loud sounds.

Thump-thump......thump-thump

Hey! What just happened? What is that thing? I don't know what it is but I'm trying to keep away from it. Do you know, mommy? Can you make it stop? Where is all that nice warm water going? Something doesn't feel right. I'm scared mommy, my heart is beating faster and I'm trying to stay away from that pointy thing.

Thump-thump-thump-thump

They've got my leg, mommy! Why are they pulling on my leg? It hurts...it hurts...why won't they stop pulling? Mommy help! I am screaming....Why don't you hear me screaming? Make them stop... please make them stop...they are pulling me apart, piece by piece.... please protect me....please make them stop....it hurts.....it hurts.....

Thump..................thump..................FLATLINE

THUMP......THUMP......FLATLINE

Oh, thank goodness the pain has stopped, mommy.

Why did that happen?

I heard someone say to make sure that **IT** is all out.

Is that my name mommy?

Did you name me **IT**?

Why did those people not like me?

Did I do something wrong?

Was I bad?

I was trying to be good for you.

Where are you, mommy?

And how did I get from your belly to Jesus' arms?

I feel safe and I feel loved, but I don't feel you, mommy.

I was created for you, mommy.

Just for you.

I was so happy to be in your belly.

I was so excited to be with you, for you to hold me, for you to love me.

Why didn't I have a choice, mommy?

It was my body and I didn't get a choice.

Those people took me away from you.

Did I matter less because I was little?

Did I matter less because I was still growing?

Why didn't my life matter, mommy?

Why didn't I matter?

I still want to be a soccer player and shoot lots of goals so you are proud of me.

Remember my little kicks to say hello?

Oh, where are you, mommy?

It's so bright here.

And so quiet.

I can't hear your voice anymore, mommy.

That always made me feel good.

And the rhythm of your heart beating helped me to fall asleep.

How will I get to sleep now, mommy?

There are so many other babies here.

I wonder if they are looking for their mommies, too?

Every time I look again, there's another baby here with me.
But, Jesus is holding us all.
He is holding us all safe in his arms.
It's time for me to go now, mommy.
But I don't feel scared anymore.
I feel loved.
I feel so loved.
Good-bye.

Every child is God's creation.
Life begins at conception.

TO FLATTEN THE CURVE

Two weeks **to flatten the curve**
Two months **to flatten the curve**
Two years **to flatten the curve**

Social distance **to flatten the curve**
Stop visiting friends **to flatten the curve**
Your grandma must die alone **to flatten the curve**

It's just a mask **to flatten the curve**
You need it to shop **to flatten the curve**
Your children must suffer hypoxia **to flatten the curve**

Just comply for now **to flatten the curve**
Just comply for a little while longer **to flatten the curve**
This is the new normal **to flatten the curve**

He must close his business **to flatten the curve**
He can't feed his family **to flatten the curve**
He lost his house **to flatten the curve**

Emergency surgery only **to flatten the curve**
She skipped her screening **to flatten the curve**
Cancer got the better of her **to flatten the curve**

School must be virtual **to flatten the curve**
They can't see their friends **to flatten the curve**
They're committing suicide **to flatten the curve**

Just buy off Amazon **to flatten the curve**
Screw the family businesses **to flatten the curve**
Bezos' was able to fund a phallic shaped rocket **to flatten the curve**

Listen to Bill Gates **to flatten the curve**
Ignore the fact that he's a eugenicist **to flatten the curve**
He's profiting off your compliance **to flatten the curve**

It's just some freedoms **to flatten the curve**
Stop being selfish **to flatten the curve**
We have to control you t**o flatten the curve**

It's just two shots **to flatten the curve**
It's just a booster **to flatten the curve**
It's just a shot every six months **to flatten the curve**

You need it to keep your job **to flatten the curve**
It causes blood clots **to flatten the curve**
You now have myocarditis **to flatten the curve**

Show us your papers **to flatten the curve**
You need it to participate in society **to flatten the curve**
It's just a microchip **to flatten the curve**

It's just a social credit score **to flatten the curve**
We must move to digital currency **to flatten the curve**
The obedient will be rewarded, the errant will be punished **to flatten the curve**

It doesn't apply to politicians **to flatten the curve**
They are the exception **to flatten the curve**
They never lost a paycheck **to flatten the curve**

STOP - BREATHE - THINK

Stop listening to the mainstream media **to flatten the curve**
Ignore hypocritical politicians **to flatten the curve**
Stop relying on pharma **to flatten the curve**

Reclaim your critical thinking skills to flatten the curve
Release your fears to flatten the curve
Do not comply to flatten the curve

TRUTH

We're back again, it makes us tired
But we'll stay in this fight
Because in the end we know
The truth WILL come to light

We give you information
One week after another
Though it seems to go in one ear
And right back out the other

Do you choose not to know or are you bought
Is the subject of our chatter
But as each week passes by
We're inclined to believe the latter

Because choosing not to know
Is certainly no excuse
And leaves us only to wonder
If you're obstinate or just obtuse

If you're being coerced by Page
To help conceal his crimes
If you need whistleblower protection
Just blink your eyes three times

Oh shoot! I forgot that was vetoed!
Even with a majority vote
Page fancies himself untouchable
And chokes democracy by the throat

These words don't apply to everyone
There are three with us on this journey
Thanks for respecting the Constitution
Tim, Mark, and Ernie

Lisa's ignorance to vaccine injury
Is a slap in the face to many
Caring for a vax injured child
Can cost families every last penny

Sam likes the Blues, galas and casinos and Kelli likes pizza
They behave like dictators on a chariot
"No mask for me, but only for thee
Because YOU'RE the proletariat"

Sam's decisions hurt many
And keep food off their table
But, he's not worried because his two jobs
Keep him financially stable

His monotone speeches
Mirror the agenda of Big Pharma
If what goes around, comes around
He's in for a lot of bad karma

The injections are experimental
Did you know? Did you agree?
Most don't even realize the trials don't end
Until 2023

They're destroying your immune system
With great advancement
Unfortunately many may soon suffer
From Antibody Dependent Enhancement

And now they're after the children
Even those as young as five
How many will suffer blood clots and strokes?
I fear that many won't survive

CDC, FDA, and Pharma
Working together in collusion
Convincing people they care for them
Though it's all one big illusion

They only care about money
And becoming more wealthy
There's no profit for them
In keeping people healthy

Fauci is a demon
I wish everyone would finally see
His funding didn't just kill puppies
It killed children with AZT

And the Mockingbird Media here on my left
Has lost all journalistic integrity
They've sold their soul for a paycheck
Like a washed up Hollywood celebrity

Agenda 2030
Has us eating crickets for food
In a one world government
All our lives will be screwed

Project Lockstep is upon us
The Great Reset has been planned
If you haven't figured it out by now
You're living in La La Land

They claim vaccine passports are needed
To end this emergency
But those of us who understand know
This all leads to digital currency

The end goal is a social credit score
So you are no longer free
You're every move will be monitored
Welcome to the CCP

We elected you to represent us
The Constitution is your guide
Our liberty is not up for debate
By that document you must abide

Because if you don't the time will come
When your actions will be undeniable
And then you'll learn what it really means
To be held criminally liable

VAX ME PFIZER ONE MORE TIME

Oh, Pfizer baby
Oh, Pfizer baby

Oh, Pfizer baby
How was I supposed to know
That you would tell me lies?
Oh, Pfizer baby
Vacantly followed the crowd flow
Programmed my immune system for demise, yeah

Show me how often it should be
Tell me, Pfizer
'Cause I need to be told now, oh, because

My ignorance
Is killing me, and I
I must confess
I still believe, still believe
The media tells me not to use my mind
Give me a booster
Vax me, Pfizer, one more time

Oh, Pfizer baby
This mask, it serves to silence me
No common sense or rationality
Oh, Pfizer baby
In fear I follow authority so blindly
It's just the way they planned it

Show me how often it should be
Tell me, Pfizer
'Cause I need to be told now, oh, because

My ignorance
Is killing me, and I
I must confess
I still believe, still believe

The media tells me not to use my mind
Give me a booster
Vax me Pfizer, one more time

Oh, Pfizer baby
Oh, Pfizer baby
Ah, yeah, yeah
Oh, Pfizer baby
How was I supposed to know?
Oh, Pfizer baby
That the CDC gets pharma's dough

I'll never confess
That my ignorance
Is killing me now
Don't you know I still believe
As clots are forming inside of me
And give me a booster
Vax me, Pfizer, one more time

My ignorance
Is killing me, and I
I must confess
I still believe, still believe
The media tells me not to use my mind
Give me a booster
Vax me Pfizer, one more time

I'll never confess
That my ignorance
Is killing me now
Don't you know I still believe
Ignoring the thousands dying suddenly
And give me a booster
Vax me, Pfizer, one more time

WAKE UP

Wake up, wake up
It's a soft kill bioweapon
Wake up, wake up
It's a culling
Abortion, child-trafficking, forced pharmaceuticals, calculated inflation, a life of servitude.
Slaves to the government, slaves to the corporations
At their will, on their terms, at our cost.
How much more will it take?
They lie to your face, they cheat and they steal.
2000 mules to cross the line.
Your best interest is not at heart.
Billions in foreign aid decided in hours, billions for your aid postponed for months
They don't give a damn about you.
History is written by the victors. Your deeds are the pen that help dictate the outcome.
Your idleness is their action.
Our children, for heaven's sake, our children, both born and unborn, are depending on us.
Our present is their future.
Wake up, wake up
It's a soft kill bioweapon
Wake up, wake up
It's a culling
Abortion, child-trafficking, forced pharmaceuticals, calculated inflation, a life of servitude.
Slaves to the government, slaves to the corporations
At their will, on their terms, at our cost.
U2 concert, Angelina Jolie visiting Ukraine in the middle of a war?
Wipe the lies from your eyes.
Protection for all borders except our own
Laundering your tax money into their pockets
All the world's a stage to further their agenda.
They incite violence to keep you distracted

Manifest racial and social contention to deflect anger away from them and towards your neighbor

Look over there, do not look here

Behind the scenes, horrendous crimes, bottomless pockets filled with blood money

Yours and your children's

Pornography in our schools, CRT fueling racism, Marxist ideologies poisoning the minds of our youth.

Keep your dirty hands off our children.

"Wokeism" is nothing more than the manifestation of a delusional mind, limited in intellectual scope, incapable of independent thought and fully dependent upon group think mentality to survive.

Stuff your "woke" in the trash

It's a pestilence on humanity and a peril to our children.

They want your body.

They want your mind.

Total control of your life

The illusion of choice

Keeping you sedated

Alcohol, sports, entertainment to pacify

To rouse when appropriate

Sway popular opinion through media influence

Slow and steady forward

Early childhood education equals early childhood indoctrination

Remove parents, remove God, remove country, remove individual accountability, remove critical thought, make them doubt themselves

Confuse the children to mold them into what they want them to be

Obedient cogs in the machine

Wake up, wake up

It's a soft kill bioweapon

Wake up, wake up

It's a culling

Abortion, child trafficking, forced pharmaceuticals, calculated inflation, a life of servitude

Slaves to the government, slaves to the corporations

At their will, on their terms, at our cost.

Wake up before it's too late

YOU KNOW YOU'RE A LIBERAL WHEN

There's a saying that goes: Liberals believe everyone should be equal at the **end** of the race while conservatives believe everyone should be equal at the **start** of the race. I feel this is an accurate assessment describing the two political leanings but, in case you have ever wondered to yourself, "Is it possible that I have allowed myself to be indoctrinated into the Left?" we'll play a little game I like to call **YOU KNOW YOU'RE A LIBERAL WHEN.** **YOU KNOW YOU'RE A LIBERAL WHEN:**

1. You believe driving an Electric Vehicle garbage truck filled with old Tesla batteries to the landfill is saving the environment.
2. You support PETA to save the puppies and Planned Parenthood to kill the babies.
3. You purchased disposable masks in bulk **and** donated to the Save The Oceans Fund.
4. You are too self-absorbed and lack the foresight to understand the future ramifications of surrendering your and your child's medical autonomy to the government.
5. You filed a sexual harrassment charge against your boss because he told you he likes your new haircut, but don't mind if your child's first grade teacher explains their sexual preferences to their class.
6. You **still** believe Disney isn't grooming children.
7. You **totally** believe your degree in Gender Studies was worth it and you wish your parents would just **shut up and stay out of the basement.**
8. You have a hammer and sickle logo on the case of your new I-Phone
9. You believe freedom of speech only applies when it reflects **your** views.
10. You have a framed photo of Fauci on your nightstand.
11. You believe the MSM relays objective and truthful reporting.
12. You **truly** believe Bill Gates is a humanitarian.
13. You oddly refuse to comprehend that the majority of immigrants coming to the U.S. for a better way of life are fleeing the socialist systems **you** wish to be implemented.
14. You wait until your child is **fifteen years old** to hold a gender reveal party.

15. It's **your turn** to do a Starbucks run for next month's ANTIFA meeting.
16. You believe the government has your best interest at heart.
17. You're an adult and you still need a "safe space."
18. You struggle with the concept of God-given freedoms because you believe **others** are responsible for your health, happiness and safety.
19. You believe in an open border policy, but live in a gated community.
20. During election cycles, a large portion of your time is spent driving around removing conservative candidate yard signs.
21. You continually refer to the U.S. as a **Democracy** when it is in fact a **Constitutional Republic.**
22. You advocate for an **inclusive** society as long as it doesn't include those you wish to **exclude.**
23. Virtue signaling with your EV trumps the guilt you feel concerning the child and slave labor used to mine the lithium for its battery.
24. You drive a Prius with a COEXIST bumper sticker, but deep down you don't mean it.
25. You see nothing wrong with a Ministry of Truth.
26. You want to erase student debt, but not for trade schools because well, those people can get jobs and pay it off themselves!
27. You're more concerned with the Johnny Depp Trial and Elon Musk buying Twitter than the **eighteen food processing plants** which burned down over the last several months.
28. Your idea of a **food supply shortage** is Trader Joe's running out of hummus.
29. You actually believe Brandon is running the show.
30. And, finally, you know you are a Liberal when you do not realize that **you** are the carbon the globalists want to eliminate.

ZEE IMPREGNATOR

It was a quiet Tuesday evening. The Liberal council members were enjoying a break from the constituents, I mean the council chambers were being renovated. Kevin found himself alone in the chambers ardently performing the Chief Deputy Clerk duties he does so well. When, out of the blue, a loud rumble and a bright beam of light tore through the time/space continuum. In that moment, Kevin found himself staring face to face with a six foot tall, seemingly genderless figure.

"Who **are** you?" Kevin asked in surprise disbelief.

"I am zee Impregnator!" replied the mysterious figure. "I haf come here mit ein varning fom za future."

"A warning from the future?" Kevin inquired.

"Ja, ein varning fom za future!"

"In za future, za lines have been crossed. Za lines have been blurred. Za lines have been erased."

"So many genders were fabricated, zat zey eventually became inconsequvential. Humans decided it vas easier to just genetically create von gender. Zat is how I, **zee Impregnator,** came into fruition."

"Zee creation of life vas schtreamlined."

"In za future, you no longer need two to tango. I, **zee Impregnator** can self-impregnate **und** give birth to a life form."

"Und, if I do not vish to procreate, I just tell myself I haf ein headache, give myself za cold shoulder, und roll over und go to sleep. I am not alvays in za mood, you know!"

"But, why are you here, Impregnator? What is your warning to us?" Kevin eagerly asked.

"Face za two gender reality now, before it's too late!" responded the Impregnator.

"Schtop traumatizing die Kinder!"

"Let girls be girls und boys be boys. Let girls be tomboys und let boys find zere vay wizout drugging und chopping zem up!"

"Schtop talking to zem about sex, let zem be kids!"

"Keep your perzonal business, perzonal!"

"Und halt mit confusing zee kids to satisfy your own pathetic dezire for acceptance!"

"Zee political Left are a bunch of sick und twisted groomers leading children down a path of doubt, self-hatred, self-destruction, und sexual perversion."

"Zey are indoctrinating zee children to become a bunch of mindless conformists."

"Because a society of mindless conformists are easy to control und manipulate und za money und za power shtays in die hands of zee elite."

"Shpeak up, shpeak out, und shpeak loud against zese tyrants or you are doomed to a life of eternal submission und slavery."

"You vill own nossing, you vill **NOT** be happy, zay vill own your body und **you vill eat zee bugs.**"

"Za future of society rests in your hands, Kevin. Go, share zese vords **und save za vorld!**"

"I will, Impregnator, I will" answered Kevin.

"Not so fast, Impregnator!" interjected Ms. Rita Days as she burst through the chamber door. "You know how things work around here...first things first! Receive, file and the county council be directed to prepare the appropriate legislation."

"Alvays za red tape wiss dies people," sighed the Impregnator. "Hasta la vista, baby!"

Printed in the United States
by Baker & Taylor Publisher Services